The Internet of Things and Business

The Internet of Things (IoT) has the potential to change how we live and work. It represents the next evolution of the computing revolution and will see the embedding of information and communication technologies within machines at home and in the workplace and across a broad range of industrial processes. The effect will be a radical restructuring of industries and business models driven by massive flows of data providing new insights into how the man-made and natural worlds work.

The Internet of Things and Business explores the business models emerging from the IoT and considers the challenges as well as the opportunities they pose to businesses around the world. Via real examples and a range of international case studies, the reader will develop an understanding of how this technology revolution will impact the business world as well as broader society.

Dr Martin De Saulles is a Principal Lecturer at the University of Brighton, UK.

Routledge Focus on Business and Management

The fields of business and management have grown exponentially as areas of research and education. This growth presents challenges for readers trying to keep up with the latest important insights. *Routledge Focus on Business and Management* presents small books on big topics and how they intersect with the world of business.

Individually, each title in the series provides coverage of a key academic topic, whilst collectively, the series forms a comprehensive collection across the business disciplines.

Careers and Talent Management
A critical perspective
Cristina Reis

Management Accounting for Beginners
Nicholas Apostolides

Truth in Marketing
A theory of claims evidence relations
Thomas Boysen Anker

A Short Guide to People Management
For HR and line managers
Antonios Panagiotakopoulous

Understanding the Born Global Firm
Neri Karra

The Internet of Things and Business
Martin De Saulles

The Search for Entrepreneurship
Simon Bridge

The Internet of Things and Business

Martin De Saulles

LONDON AND NEW YORK

First published 2017
by Routledge
2 Park Square, Milton Park, Abingdon, Oxon OX14 4RN

and by Routledge
605 Third Avenue, New York, NY 10017

Routledge is an imprint of the Taylor & Francis Group, an informa business

British Library Cataloguing in Publication Data
A catalogue record for this book is available from the British Library

Library of Congress Cataloging in Publication Data
A catalog record for this book has been requested

ISBN: 978-1-138-68922-0 (hbk)
ISBN: 978-1-315-53784-9 (ebk)

Typeset in Times New Roman
by Apex CoVantage, LLC

For Helen

Contents

Figures

Acknowledgements

The idea for this book emerged from my long-standing interest in organisations' application and deployment of new technologies. This started with my postgraduate study at the Science Policy Research Unit (SPRU) at the University of Sussex in the 1990s followed by work as a researcher and analyst at Mercer Management Consulting in London and then Analysys in Cambridge. I owe a lot to my PhD supervisor, Professor Robin Mansell, who patiently steered me through my studies, and the colleagues at Mercer and Analysys who helped me apply my research skills to the business world. Finally, I would like to thank my colleagues and the students I have taught over the previous decade at the University of Brighton. Working with such a group of intelligent and thoughtful people every day is a privilege.

1 Introduction

> "Every great movement must experience three stages: ridicule, discussion, adoption."
>
> – John Stuart Mill

The Internet of Things (IoT) has the potential to change how we live and work in ways greater than the internet has up to this point. Thus far, the internet has changed how we communicate and access information. Email, instant messaging and social media have accelerated the speed with which we share information with friends, family and colleagues, and the World Wide Web (WWW) has provided a global platform for freely publishing information to the world. However, while these innovations have made significant impacts on the publishing, communications and entertainment sectors, industries in other sectors have been far less affected. The application of computing technologies within businesses has changed back-office processes to an extent in terms of operating efficiencies, but most industries still develop and deliver their goods and services in much the same way they did 30 years ago. The IoT is the next evolution of the computing revolution and will see the embedding of information and communication technologies (ICTs) within machines at home and in the workplace and across a broad range of industrial processes. The effect will be a radical restructuring of industries and business models driven by massive flows of data providing new insights into how the man-made and natural worlds work. New companies will emerge to capitalise on this data while established ones will need to adapt the way they operate or face extinction in the same way that steam, electricity and the internal combustion engine rendered obsolete old ways of working. Within a few years many billions of new devices will be connected via the IoT, generating trillions of dollars of value to businesses and national economies (Gartner, 2014; Manyika et al., 2015; Norton, 2015).

So what is the Internet of Things? Gartner, the technology analyst company, defines the IoT as:

> the network of physical objects that contain embedded technology to communicate and sense or interact with their internal states or the external environment.
>
> (Gartner, 2016)

Although this may sound like a rather dry definition for an area of technology which promises so much, it does encapsulate the form and function of the IoT at a high level. The key words to take away from the definition are "network", "embedded", "communicate", "sense" and "external environment". Embedding networked sensors into everyday objects and ones yet to come to market will provide businesses, as well as public bodies, with almost unimaginable quantities of data. The application of machine learning and artificial intelligence (AI) software to analyse and make sense of this data will herald a new wave of innovation in business processes and industrial organisation. Other definitions for the IoT exist; network technology giant Cisco talks about the "Internet of Everything" while some companies talk about machine-to-machine (M2M) innovations. These are explored in more detail in Chapter 2, but the key point to realise is that the IoT is not a single technology, but a broad range of technologies which are coming together in synergy where the whole is greater than the sum of its parts. This book explores the impact that the IoT is having on the business world and considers some of the key companies driving this revolution, the business models which are emerging and where it is likely to lead. This is a fast-moving sector with new players and technologies emerging all the time, which makes writing a book on the subject difficult. However, although up-to-the-minute examples have been used to illustrate what is happening in the IoT world, the core models and frameworks discussed will provide a solid foundation for the reader to make sense of this revolution as it unfolds.

Chapter 2 considers the origins of the IoT and the technologies which have come together to form its foundations. In Chapter 3, the core drivers from the supply and demand side are examined to explain why the IoT is developing in its current form. Chapter 4 goes into detail on the key companies from across the technology spectrum which are shaping the IoT. Chapter 5 explores the business models of these companies and considers the broader impact on where value is likely to be generated in an IoT world. In Chapter 6, the main challenges facing companies and broader society from a pervasive IoT are examined, including the issues of privacy, security and regulation. Finally, in Chapter 7, the future of the IoT is considered in terms of likely business winners, emerging technologies and the impact of the IoT on the world of work.

References

Gartner, 2014. *Gartner Says 4.9 Billion Connected.* [online]. Available at: www.gartner.com/newsroom/id/2905717.

Gartner, 2016. *IT Glossary.* [online]. Available at: www.gartner.com/it-glossary/internet-of-things/.

Manyika, J., Chui, M., Bisson, P., Woetzel, J., Dobbs, R., Bughin, J. and Aharon, D., 2015. *The Internet of Things: Mapping the Value beyond the Hype*. San Francisco, CA: McKinsey & Company.

Norton, S., 2015. *Internet of Things Market to Reach $1.7 Trillion by 2020: IDC.* Available at: www.idc.com/getdoc.jsp?containerId=prUS25658015.

2 The origins of the IoT

Before exploring in detail the implications of the IoT for business as well as broader society, it is important to understand the origins of this technology revolution. As with all new computing and communication technologies, the IoT is built on a range of innovations stretching back to the nineteenth century, when it first became possible to remotely monitor environmental conditions. This chapter considers these developments and the role they played in creating the IoT.

The ability to remotely monitor the environment and/or control devices at long distance is known as telemetry. The first telemetry system is reported to have been in early nineteenth-century Russia, where the Russian army remotely detonated mines to slow down the invading French. A system closer to more modern telemetry systems designed to relay information from remote locations can be traced back to 1845, when a data transmission circuit was established between the tsar's Winter Palace and Russian army headquarters to exchange logistics information (Mayo-Wells, 1963). In the twentieth century, telemetry became widely accepted for use in power-generating plants to remotely measure power outputs of individual power stations and loading on transmission networks. These landline-based systems used fixed wires and were rolled out to chemical-processing plants, oil wells and petroleum pipelines to transmit operating information. The first wireless telemetry systems were used in weather balloons, where the design emphasis was on size and power consumption. This was then incorporated into aircraft to monitor flight performance and removed the need for pilots to make measurements themselves (Foster, 1965). The Second World War accelerated the deployment of wireless telemetry systems in aircraft, but also in the emerging rocket-based weapons being developed in Germany. These technologies fed into the American space program and were pivotal in getting men on the moon.

By the mid-twentieth century, the value of telemetry systems and, more specifically, the data which flowed across them was becoming apparent in both commercial and government spheres. However, one of the limitations of these systems was their proprietary nature, with systems being developed for very specific purposes and using a disparate range of hardware, software and transmission protocols. While the systems were generally good at providing data for the narrow purpose for which they had been built, they had little or no value beyond that. Later in the twentieth century, these systems became more sophisticated and the term *machine-to-machine* (M2M) emerged to describe a broad range of systems and networks which were being deployed across industrial sectors.

At the same time, the internet was taking shape and by the turn of the millennium had become established as the primary network for exchanging digital data streams across and between individuals, corporations and the public sector. Built around the TCP/IP open protocol, the internet allowed anyone or anything, using this protocol, to connect with each other and exchange digital bits which might be reconstructed to form text, images, video or music. The non-proprietary and open nature of the internet was the key factor in its rapid dominance over proprietary networks such as CompuServe, AOL and Prodigy. The open nature of the internet as a platform for innovation encourages third parties, whether large corporations or students in dorm rooms, to develop content and applications which can sit on top of this network. Permission is not required from any 'internet authority' to create the next Facebook or Google. Obviously, there are barriers to entry based around the notion of network externalities or network effects which give established players such as Facebook an inherent advantage, but the internet itself is still, for the moment at least, an open platform.

As we saw in the introductory chapter, the IoT encompasses a range of information and communication technologies (ICTs), as well as activities such as data analytics. The development of telematics and then M2M systems has proven the business case for data-gathering and -monitoring networks, and the mass deployment of the internet has provided a robust and cost-efficient backbone across which to transmit the data. Alongside the development and adoption of the internet has been the pervasive diffusion of computing by both businesses and individuals. The computing industry has seen a series of revolutions, first with the rise of mainframe computing in the 1950s and 1960s followed by mini computers in the 1970s. In the 1980s and 1990s, personal computers (PCs) introduced end users to the computing revolution and provided the foundations, along with mobile phones, for the smartphone revolution. By the end of 2015, it was estimated there were 3.2 billion smartphones users around the world (43% of the global population), and it is forecast that this number will rise to 6.3 billion users by 2021 (81% of the global population) (Qureshi, 2016). Smartphones are no longer a high-end luxury for wealthy individuals, but are becoming pervasive in developing countries as well. The attractions of having a connected computer which can fit in your pocket are obvious, and such devices are becoming the entry point into computing for generations of consumers in countries where the personal computing revolution has been skipped for a mobile computing one. This is being made possible through the economies of scale enabled by the mass production of smartphones with unsubsidised handsets available for less than $20. A side effect of this revolution is the industry which has emerged, particularly in China and Southeast Asia, producing smartphone components such as sensors, accelerometers, radio chips and microprocessors. These have become commodity items and are one of the enablers of the IoT which relies on cheap components to produce this next generation of embedded and pervasive computing devices.

The notion of computing devices becoming embedded in our daily lives emerged once PCs had begun to appear on office desks and in homes. In 1991, Mark Weiser, then head of the Computer Science Laboratory at the Xerox Palo Alto Research Center,[1] claimed that:

> The most profound technologies are those that disappear. They weave themselves into the fabric of everyday life until they are indistinguishable from it.
>
> (Weiser, 1991, p.94)

Weiser's prescient paper anticipated the emergence of embedded, intelligent devices and saw beyond the PC as the dominant paradigm for how we interact with computers. While new technologies have emerged since 1991 which Weiser could not have anticipated, his vision of a world where intelligence is built into everyday objects to create an environment of 'ubiquitous computing' describes many of the features of the emerging IoT. According to Gravely (2015), the first what he terms "internet appliance" was a Coke machine in the early 1980s at Carnegie Mellon University which allowed staff to check via the internet whether the machine had cold drinks so they did not have to make a wasted journey down the hallway. However, it took until the late 1990s for a more refined description of what a world of ubiquitous computing might look like when Kevin Ashton, then a brand manager at Proctor and Gamble (P&G), saw the potential for RFID chips to streamline the vast supply chains which companies like P&G were part of. Kellmereit and Obodovski (2013) sum up Ashton's vision for an "Internet of Things":[2]

> Information about objects – like Gillette razor blades or Pantene shampoos – would be stored on the internet, and the smart tag on the object would just point to this information.
>
> (Kellmereit and Obodovski, 2013, p.17)

Reflecting on his original vision 10 years later, Ashton (2009) argues that the core benefit of a fully developed Internet of Things would be computers gathering information from RFID- and sensor-enabled objects for themselves rather than relying on humans to input the information. People, he claims, are not as efficient as computers at collecting, managing and inputting data, and by bypassing humans we may be creating a new revolution greater than that enabled by the internet.

This idea has been taken up by a number of writers, researchers and analysts (Anderson and Rainie, 2014; Bauer, Patel and Veira, 2014; Berthelsen, 2015; Greenfield, 2006; Kellmereit and Obodovski, 2013; Meunier et al., 2014) over the previous decade to the extent that a broad consensus now exists as to what the IoT comprises and what its potential is. As with any new technology there is always the risk of it being over-hyped by enthusiastic vendors, analysts and commentators. Gartner acknowledges this and in 2015 placed the IoT at the "Peak of Inflated Expectations" in terms of its path to diffusion (Gartner, 2015). However, it should be noted that this stage precedes, for those emerging technologies which are ultimately successful, the journey to the "Slope of Enlightenment" and then the "Plateau of Productivity" if one accepts Gartner's model of technology adoption.

There are strong indicators that the IoT is not a transient technology which will go the way of previous over-hyped innovations that never met with market success. We can see that the enabling infrastructure is already largely in place with pervasive wireless broadband, cheap computing components and backend infrastructure to manage the data. The success of the smartphone as a communications and computing device demonstrates a demand from users for any technology which helps make sense of our environment. There are also the massive investments from large corporations such as GE, Bosch, Microsoft and Amazon in building out the infrastructure needed to manage the massive data streams flowing from the billions of connected devices already forming a nascent IoT. Whether this new computing and communications revolution is called the IoT by historians in decades to come is of little importance. The reality is that the world has already started on an unstoppable journey to connect billions of everyday objects to the internet which is opening up new and yet to be discovered opportunities for businesses to profit from.

Notes

1 The Xerox Palo Alto Research Center has been at the heart of a number of the most important innovations behind the success of the PC revolution, including the graphical user interface (GUI), the mouse and the laser printer.

2 Kevin Ashton is credited with coining the phrase 'Internet of Things' in 1999 when he made a presentation to the P&G board outlining his thoughts on the application of RFID chips to the company's supply chain.

References

Anderson, J. and Rainie, L., 2014. *The Internet of Things Will Thrive by 2025*. Pew Research Center. [online]. Available at: www.pewinternet.org/2014/05/14/internet-of-things/.

Ashton, K., 2009. That 'internet of things' thing. *RFID Journal*, 22(7), pp.97–114.

Bauer, H., Patel, M. and Veira, J., 2014. The Internet of Things: Sizing Up the Opportunity. *McKinsey & Company*. [online]. Available at: www.mckinsey.com/industries/high-tech/our-insights/the-internet-of-things-sizing-up-the-opportunity.

Berthelsen, E., 2015. Enterprise IoT Will Disrupt Your Industry. *Machina Research*. [online]. Available at: https://machinaresearch.com/report/enterprise-iot-will-disrupt-your-industry/.

Foster, L.E., 1965. *Telemetry Systems*. New York: John Wiley & Sons.

Gartner, 2015. *Gartner's 2015 Hype Cycle for Emerging Technologies Identifies the Computing Innovations That Organizations Should Monitor*. [online]. Available at: www.gartner.com/newsroom/id/3114217.

Gravely, S., 2015. *The Internet of Things and Healthcare*. Atlanta, GA: Troutman Sanders LLP.

Greenfield, A., 2006. *Everyware: The Dawning Age of Ubiquitous Computing*. Berkeley, CA: New Riders.

Kellmereit, D. and Obodovski, D., 2013. *The Silent Intelligence – The Internet of Things*. 1st ed. San Francisco, CA: DND Ventures.

Mayo-Wells, W.J., 1963. The origins of space telemetry. *Technology and Culture*, 4(4), pp.499–514.

Meunier, F., Wood, A., Weiss, K., Huberty, K. and Flannery, S., 2014. *The 'Internet of Things' Is Now: Connecting the Real Economy*. Blue Papers. New York: Morgan Stanley.

Qureshi, R., 2016. Ericsson Mobility Report. *Ericsson*. [online]. Available at: www.ericsson.com/mobility-report.

Weiser, M., 1991. The computer for the 21st century. *Scientific American*, 265(3), pp.94–104.

3 IoT drivers

Introduction

Innovations and new technologies are usually the results of endeavours by multiple actors who build on the capabilities of existing technologies. As we saw in the previous chapter, the internet is a good example of a technological platform which emerged from publicly funded research, government research priorities, open communications standards and protocols and an underpinning physical network managed by private operators. The IoT, although a less well-defined system than the internet, is no different in that whatever shape it ultimately takes, it will be the result of research and investments by a wide range of organisations, public and private. The days when single inventors and entrepreneurs such as Bell, Edison and Marconi in the nineteenth century could launch revolutionary innovations on the world from their laboratories are long gone. While some may argue that Bill Gates, Steve Jobs and Mark Zuckerberg are modern-day equivalents of their nineteenth-century forebears, the modern world is a far more complex place than that which Alexander Graham Bell faced when he invented the telephone. Although Bill Gates is rightly seen as a pioneer of PC operating software, Microsoft would have been nothing without the hardware platform of the PC developed by IBM and Intel. Steve Jobs' Apple computer can certainly be credited with transforming the way we interact with PCs, but his use of a mouse with a graphical user interface (GUI) was the result of innovations developed by the Xerox Palo Alto Research Center a decade earlier. While it is true that Mark Zuckerberg's Facebook is regularly used by more than 1 billion people, without the internet, the World Wide Web and ubiquitous connectivity it would never have been possible.

This interconnectedness of modern technology systems is a shaping force of the IoT. For the IoT to deliver on its potential as outlined in the previous chapter, it needs to be able to share data across multiple networks and with a wide range of stakeholders. Email was a key driver in the early consumer and business adoption of the internet because it allowed users to communicate with each other independent of which company provided their internet connectivity. This was possible because the underlying standards and protocols facilitating email are not proprietary. Similarly, the WWW became a dominant platform for the publishing of content across the internet because it relied on free and open protocols which were not owned by any single company.

This chapter explores the key dynamics driving the development and adoption of IoT products, systems and services. It will consider those drivers which are pushing the development of the IoT and those pull factors which are shaping its adoption. By looking at historical examples of open and closed communication systems we will see how different approaches often have very different results. This chapter will conclude by examining some of the technological, social, economic and legal barriers which stand in the way of a potentially pervasive IoT.

The role of platforms

The importance of platforms in the development and diffusion of new technologies has already been mentioned in this book. While the term is often used in the context of technological innovation, it is important to define what it means, particularly with reference to the IoT. In their investigation of the role of platforms in product development, technology strategy and industrial economics, Baldwin and Woodard (2009) define a platform as

> a set of stable components that supports variety and evolvability in a system by constraining the linkages among the other components. (p.19)

Important in this definition is the notion that constraints imposed by the platform can help the system to successfully develop and evolve. Gawer and Cusumano (2002) demonstrated this in their detailed analysis of how Intel, Microsoft and Cisco used technology platforms to dominate their market sectors. In the case of Intel, the authors show how the company led the development of the personal computer (PC) platform throughout the 1980s and 1990s by bringing together a range of other hardware and software companies to create a platform architecture which combined stability with enough flexibility to encourage innovation. The PC platform conformed to Baldwin and Woodard's definition by offering stability and the right balance of constraint and flexibility. This can be placed in contrast with the approach of Apple Computers in the same period, which adopted a very different, proprietary model whereby only Apple, with some limited exceptions in the early 1990s, designed and manufactured its computers. The end result of this was that by the mid-1990s the company was almost bankrupt and had only a tiny share of the PC market.

However, although Intel and Microsoft may have won the PC wars of the 1990s with a more flexible computing platform than Apple, it should not be thought that theirs was an open platform. Intel maintained control of the hardware aspects of the platform while Microsoft controlled its operating system. Third parties were encouraged to develop components and software to run on the platform, but only within the rules set by Intel and Microsoft, which were designed to drive the sales of Intel's processors and Microsoft's software. Greenstein (2009) notes that this approach was in stark contrast to the development of the internet, which was not dominated by the commercial interests of any companies. The body tasked in the 1990s with expanding the capabilities and reach of the internet, the Internet Engineering Task Force (IETF), required its members, where possible, to develop and use non-proprietary technologies and standards. The end result of this was a communications platform which was based on open standards and which was not dominated by any commercial interests. Zittrain (2008) shows how the evolution of the internet into an open platform for innovation conflicted with the telecommunication networks of companies such as AT&T and the regional Bell operating companies in the United States. Their platforms were tightly controlled and had evolved very little over the decades in the services they offered to customers. This control extended to the operators usually being the sole providers of the hardware such as handsets which connected to their networks. As Zittrain points out, AT&T was not averse to bringing legal actions against any third parties which developed and tried to sell alternative handsets.

Before the mass adoption of the internet by households from the late 1990s, other information services existed which could be delivered via the telephone networks. These included CompuServe, America Online, Prodigy and Genie. In the United Kingdom, a service called Prestel was offered by the British Post Office, and in France, a far more successful offering called Minitel was provided by France Telecom. Each of the services differed in the content it offered and the degree to which proprietary hardware was required. Typical services included messaging capabilities to other subscribers and access to news feeds and discussion fora. However, a core weakness of all the systems was an inability for them to communicate with each other. A CompuServe subscriber, for example, could send messages to other CompuServe subscribers, but not to someone on the Prodigy network. Another limitation was the availability of third-party content which was controlled by the network operators. As internet connectivity amongst households and businesses began to take off in the late 1990s, some of these services offered gateways for their subscribers to the internet, but their proprietary platforms began to wither as users moved out of their walled gardens and into the wild frontier of the open internet.

So what does this all mean for the evolution of the IoT? Will it be possible for a small number of corporations to dominate this emerging market in the same way that Intel and Microsoft did in the PC sector? Would this approach stifle innovation in the same way that the telecom operators did for much of the twentieth century with their closed networks and resistance to allowing third parties to provide complementary services? Does the IoT need to be based on open standards and protocols in the same way as the internet itself? Are there modern-day IoT equivalents of CompuServe and Minitel which, while operating successfully today, are destined to be swept away by a platform which has yet to emerge? While it is impossible to answer these questions with certainty, an examination of the platforms and standards which are emerging in the IoT-enabled smart home may give us some clues.

IoT smart home hardware includes thermostats, smoke alarms, video cameras, fridges and door locks, amongst other devices which monitor their environment and allow users to remotely control households. By their nature these devices need to communicate with other equipment to share data. This is normally done wirelessly, and it is here we can see how different standards and platforms are emerging. Established communication protocols for smart home devices include ZigBee, WeMo and Z-Wave. According to Parrish (2015), the Z-Wave Alliance claims to have more than 1,300 certified devices which use its wireless standard. However, it is a proprietary standard which makes those devices incompatible with devices using WeMo or ZigBee. ZigBee is widely used across a range of household devices, including GE and Philips smart lighting solutions, while WeMo uses the standard 2.4 GHz Wi-Fi frequency to communicate. Each has its advantages in terms of wireless range and power consumption, but none of these standards has established a dominant position in the market for smart home devices and solutions. More recent entrants to this market include Google with its Thread communications standard and Brillo IoT operating system, Apple with its HomeKit platform and Samsung's SmartThings IoT hub. These systems can, to varying degrees, work with established communication protocols and platforms, but they illustrate a fluid and dynamic market for smart home products and solutions.

IoT drivers – supply side

Markets for new technologies are usually driven by a combination of the companies and organisations behind the technologies trying to persuade potential users to adopt them, as well as demand factors from those with a need for what the technology can deliver. This section looks at the forces pushing IoT products and services onto the market.

To some degree it is an accidental confluence of circumstances and technologies which is driving innovation in the IoT sector. Much as the industrial revolution of the late eighteenth and early nineteenth centuries came about through innovations in iron and steel production, steam power, transportation and cheap labour, so the IoT's foundations are based on recent developments in the technology sector. According to Bellini and colleagues (2014), these developments include low-cost sensors, smartphones, cheap processing, cheap bandwidth, near-pervasive wireless coverage, big data and IPv6. Partly driven by the mass adoption of smartphones, sensors such as accelerometers, GPS chips and cameras have dramatically fallen in price over the previous decade, reducing the price of key IoT components. Via apps, smartphones also make good controllers for IoT devices such as fitness trackers, smart watches and smart home installations. The rollout of 3G and 4G cellular networks across most of the developed world, as well as cheap, fixed broadband connections for households with Wi-Fi capabilities, allows resilient wireless connectivity for the IoT. Big data in the context of the IoT, Bellini and colleagues (2014) argue, refers to the backend infrastructure offered by a number of companies which provides low-cost but powerful facilities for storing and processing the large quantities of data thrown off by IoT devices. Finally, IPv6 is the successor Internet Protocol to IPv4 which can only provide around 4.3 billion IP addresses and has effectively reached this capacity. Clearly for a world in which technology analysts IDC (2014) predict more than 28 billion connected IoT devices by 2020, a new protocol was needed. IPv6 provides 3.4×10^{38} addresses, an almost unimaginably large number and more than enough for at least the next several decades.

While these innovations are providing a technological foundation for the IoT, a major push in developing actual products and solutions is coming from a wide range of computing and communication companies. As we saw in the previous chapter, computing technologies tend to emerge in waves as the lifecycles of previous computing generations mature and are replaced or supplemented by new generations. Mainframe computers and then mini computers were the dominant platforms from the 1950s to the 1970s. By the 1980s, PCs started to appear on desktops and took away much of the processing which had been done centrally on the larger machines. Laptops added a degree of portability for computer users from the 1990s, and more recently tablets and smartphones have become the primary computing device for many users. This has been aided by the internet and cloud computing which removes much of the processing from devices and onto remote servers. Meunier and colleagues (2014) believe the IoT represents the next computing revolution, as do many technology companies eager to stake a claim in this emerging market. In 2015, IBM announced it was investing more than $10 billion and intended to hire 2,000 new employees for its IoT Business Unit (MarketWatch, 2015). Communications equipment manufacturer Cisco estimates that the global IoT marketplace will be worth $19 trillion by 2024 (Cisco, 2014) and is forming alliances with other technology companies to develop IoT services. Samsung, a manufacturer of household and personal electronics from washing machines to smartphones, hopes that its SmartThings Hub will act as a unifying device for managing a range of IoT-enabled hardware from other manufacturers as well as its own. The SmartThings Hub is able to communicate across a number of the different protocols described earlier and, in theory at least, to remove the need for multiple hubs and gateways in the home. According to Gibbs:

> Samsung has also pledged to make 100% of its devices, from TVs and sound systems to washing machines and fridges, internet connected within five years, which will all integrate into the SmartThings Hub.
>
> (Gibbs, 2015)

Google is adopting a different approach to building its smart home IoT platform with the development of Android-based Brillo, which it hopes IoT device manufacturers will use as the operating system for their products. Providing a software platform based on open standards has certainly worked well for Google with Android as, by the middle of 2016, it commanded an 84% share of the global smartphone operating system market (IDC, 2016). Unsurprisingly, Apple is also attempting to stake a claim in the smart home sector with its HomeKit platform which allows users to control a range of compatible devices from Apple and third parties with their iPhones and iPads. This strategy is an attempt by Apple to place its existing products at the centre of the smart home and, by extension, drive sales of its very profitable iPhones and iPads. While Google's Android operating system may be the dominant platform for smartphones, Apple takes the majority of profits from the sector. Even though only 14% of smartphones were iPhones in 2015 according to IDC (2015), they accounted for 92% of all profits in the sector (Ovide and Wakabayashi, 2015).

In identifying the key drivers from the supply side which are driving the IoT sector we also need to look beyond companies such as Google, IBM, Cisco and Apple which are developing the underlying technologies and standards. In the context of the smart home, there are a number of companies offering existing products and services to households which see the IoT as a way to deepen relationships with their customers by embedding these new technologies into traditionally 'non-smart' things. In the United Kingdom, utility company British Gas launched its smart thermostat, Hive, in 2013 and by mid-2015 claimed more than 200,000 customers. According to Gilbert (2015), this makes British Gas the largest connected home provider in the United Kingdom. However, British Gas is not restricting its IoT initiative to the thermostat, and through its Honeycomb IoT software platform it hopes other companies will make compatible devices to run over its system. This could be seen as either an offensive move by British Gas to branch out into new markets or a defensive move to protect the company from being disintermediated by new entrants such as Google and Apple. Even the market for door locks is facing challenges from new IoT companies. The mechanisms for locking doors with keys has barely changed in centuries, but embedding sensors and a degree of computational intelligence into the locks is allowing us to open doors with our smartphones. Technology research company NextMarket Insights estimates that the global market for smart locks will grow from $261 million in 2014 to $3.6 billion by 2019 (NextMarket Insights, 2014). As a result, established lock manufacturers such as Yale and Schlage are developing smart locks and entry mechanisms to ensure they are not left behind in this new market.

Clearly, some very large technology companies are pushing a range of IoT devices, services and platforms. Some are doing this in attempts to establish proprietary standards which may drive extraordinary profits in the same way that Microsoft was able to do for the PC in the 1980s and 1990s. Others see the IoT as a way to drive sales of established and new products whether these are washing machines, fridges or smartphones. Behind these companies are others which see the IoT as driving demand for their data storage, analytical and consulting services. However, markets for new technologies driven primarily from the supply side and based on inflated claims for the potential of the new products and services are unlikely to succeed. We saw in the previous chapter that in 2015, Gartner placed the IoT at the top of the Peak of Inflated Expectations as part of its annual technology Hype Cycle analysis. This does not mean the company believes the IoT has no future, but that if it is to proceed successfully to the Slope of Enlightenment, then the companies offering IoT solutions must deliver products and services which meet real market needs. In the late 1990s, many technology companies, including IBM and consulting firms such as Accenture and PWC, claimed to offer 'knowledge management' solutions to companies wishing to apply computing power to the management of intellectual assets residing amongst their employees. There was a widespread belief that computers could manage more than just basic information but could also act as repositories of valuable, firm-specific knowledge which could provide a competitive advantage. This promise was never effectively delivered by those vendors with marketing claims and customer expectations far exceeding the abilities of the technology (Wilson, 2002). While there is always a danger that the IoT goes the way of knowledge management and never emerges from the Trough of Disillusionment, it seems unlikely that this will happen. The underpinning, established technologies described previously and the well-funded companies developing them provide a strong foundation for a dynamic and successful sector to emerge. Also, as we will see in the next section, there is strong demand from current and potential IoT customers across a range of industrial sectors creating an enthusiastic market for suppliers.

IoT drivers – demand side

According to Evans and Annunziata (2012), the IoT could add between $10 trillion and $15 trillion to global GDP by 2032. Much of this, they claim, will come from cost savings to industry brought about by the application of IoT technologies to industrial processes. This has already begun in many industry sectors as the application of smart and connected sensors across a range of activities is producing operating information at unprecedented rates. In the oil and gas (O&G) industry, for example, the internal data being generated in the field by a large O&G company exceeds 1.5 terabytes a day (Slaughter, Bean and Mittal, 2015). According to the authors:

> IoT applications could reduce production and lifting costs by more than $500 million of a large O&G integrated company with annual production of 270 million barrels.
>
> (Slaughter, Bean and Mittal, 2015, p.8)

In the United Kingdom, utility company Thames Water has installed sensors across its water storage and supply networks which, coupled with a backend analytics platform which can process the information in real time, allows the company to predict equipment failures and respond more quickly to sudden events such as leaks and flooding (O'Halloran and Kvochko, 2015). It is the ability to remotely monitor equipment, receive real-time data from these sensors and have processing capabilities to make sense of the data which is driving many traditional industrial companies to invest in IoT technologies. As with Thames Water, the use of software to predict equipment breakdowns reduces and sometimes removes the need for expensive engineers to routinely check equipment whether there is a problem with it.

The domestic energy supply market is a good example of where consumer-facing IoT technologies are linking back to industry-focused IoT infrastructure.

This is where the smart home meets the 'smart grid'. Electricity distribution has changed little over the past 80 years with large power stations generating power that is then fed out to households via a grid of powerlines. While this system reliably provides us with electricity on demand in our homes, it is not necessarily the most efficient way of utilising scarce energy resources. As our demand for electricity varies across the day and the time of year, the generating plants need to provide more energy than is required to ensure a continuous supply. Power stations can be powered up and down, but this takes time and is one of the reasons why electricity is usually cheaper late at night when consumer demand is lower and there is excess capacity. This centralised model is being challenged by the rise of domestic solar generation, local wind farms and biomass plants, as well as other localised initiatives. There are obvious environmental benefits to these changes, but moving away from a centrally controlled model raises problems with making sure electricity gets to the right people at the right time. Smart meters linked to IoT-enabled domestic thermostats provide a back channel of information to the power companies and allow them to better utilise energy resources. When household devices such as washing machines, dishwashers and water heaters are also connected to this network, they can be remotely controlled to ensure they make best use of excess electricity capacity. According to Meunier and colleagues (2014):

> In the UK, domestic consumers are currently wasting up to 20% on their heating and cooling bills due to inefficient scheduling, according to Nest. Substantial savings are also likely to be achieved with other devices, such as lighting, household appliances etc.
>
> (Meunier et al., 2014, p.39)

For energy companies and consumers, this has the potential to be a win-win scenario as bills are reduced, but so are the operating costs incurred by the generators.

Another sector pioneering the implementation of IoT solutions is the insurance industry. More than 90% of road accidents are the result of human error with certain classes of driver more likely than others to be involved in those accidents (KPMG, 2015). The availability of low-cost, reliable GPS chips and almost ubiquitous mobile broadband in most developed economies is transforming the way insurers calculate risk and the behaviour of drivers. Placing GPS-enabled trackers in cars allows insurance companies to monitor the driving behaviour of their customers. The data collected include miles driven, speeds, braking, acceleration, time of driving, places visited and style of driving. From this data, insurers are able to tailor premiums based on driver behaviour. In the United Kingdom, this has led to a 20% reduction in accidents amongst young drivers whose cars have had these trackers installed, as well as substantially reducing premiums for drivers who demonstrate safe driving (Insley, 2012). As with the energy example cited earlier, this technology has benefits for both insurers and their customers. It has been calculated that the application of smart sensors and trackers to cars could save insurers in the United States almost $75 billion in claim pay-outs by 2040 (KPMG, 2015).

Even a sector as established and traditional as agriculture is driving the adoption of IoT solutions. Sensors in fields can track moisture levels, temperature, soil acidity and fertiliser levels and report these data back to farmers to allow for more accurate and efficient land management. Combining this data with GPS-based controllers on tractors and, increasingly, autonomous farm vehicles which can apply fertiliser, huge cost savings can be made. In some cases, machinery and other input costs can be reduced by up to 75% (Zarco-Tejada, Hubbard and Loudjani, 2014).

Through these examples, we can see the potential for huge cost savings from the application of IoT technologies and services to a range of industries. The attraction of this to companies is obvious and will be a major driver of initial adoption. In his broad-ranging and influential research on the adoption of innovations over almost five decades, Rogers (2003) demonstrated the key factors which drive successful adoption. One of the most important of these was that the innovation must demonstrate a relative advantage over existing ways of doing things. Clearly, the IoT offers significant benefits in terms of efficiencies for the supply side as well as for the demand side in terms of lower prices. We have seen that the underpinning technologies are being put into place to enable the IoT to become a reality and that this is coupled with real demand for the resulting services. However, there are issues which need to be considered in this context and which could act as barriers to the mass adoption of the IoT. The next section will examine these, their likely impact and how they might be overcome.

Barriers to adoption

Technical barriers

We saw earlier in this chapter how different and often competing standards from a variety of industry players and consortia are creating a fluid and fragmented market for IoT products and services. It is likely that this will settle down as a small number of standards and industry players begin to dominate sectors of the IoT marketplace. Markets for new, innovative technologies are usually characterised by this instability as new entrants rush in to capitalise on an emerging trend and try to establish strong, defensible positions. The initial focus of activity by these early innovators is on making changes to the products or services they offer as they learn about market preferences and the capabilities of the new technology. As the new technology matures and a dominant design emerges, the focus of innovation switches to improving the processes by which the product is produced. This was the case with the first automobiles at the beginning of the twentieth century when a number of designs for the power and steering mechanisms competed with each other (Abernathy and Utterback, 1978). These included steam, electric and petrol-based engines while steering took the form of tillers, levers and wheels. Eventually the internal combustion engine and steering wheel format won the day, and the focus of producers then switched to how the cars were made. Henry Ford pioneered cost savings through economies of scale and a moving production line, and the modern car industry was born. Mass adoption of the automobile as a form of personal transport became possible once the prices were low enough for the average consumer and an infrastructure of suitable roads and petrol stations were built out. In the case of the IoT, trying to anticipate a dominant design in the same way we can see how a successful configuration of technologies and designs led to the modern motor car is not so easy. This is largely because the IoT is not such a homogenous entity as the car but is rather a diverse set of technologies, standards and services. However, we can look for dominant formats in terms of the underpinning technologies, the software running on them and the standards by which they communicate. We have seen that these are all still in a state of flux, but, for a truly interconnected IoT, a dominant design in terms of this configuration will need to emerge. End users, whether domestic consumers or industrial purchasers, will be reluctant to invest in systems which they fear may become obsolete or will not be able to communicate with other IoT devices.

A feature of many information systems is the impact that network effects can have on their success or failure. Network effects or network externalities relate to the way an information system can increase in value to its users as more members join it. A telephone network is of little value to anyone when only a handful of people connect to it. However, as more people join, it raises the number of possible connections its users can make and creates a virtuous circle of increasing value. Facebook benefits from network effects as new members are very likely to know people already on the network. Conversely, companies seeking to create alternative social networks are penalised by this effect as there is little incentive for users to join a new network when their friends and family are already on Facebook. IoT platforms such as those Google, Apple, Samsung and IBM are developing are subject to similar forces and whichever companies emerge as winners, network effects will play a key role. Equipment suppliers will be drawn to platforms which have the largest user bases and consumers will gravitate to those systems which have the largest supporting ecosystems of apps, hardware and information services.

Economic barriers

New technologies are typically expensive to produce as sales are low and economies of scale have not had a chance to permeate through the supply chain. The first mobile phone was sold in 1984 for $4,000, which would equate to more than $9,000 in 2016 money (Wolpin, 2014). It took more than 15 years for it to become a product for the masses when prices fell to affordable levels. For consumer-facing IoT products and services such as wearables and home monitoring equipment, price will be an important factor. However, the prices of components which make up many of these devices are already very low due to their established use in smartphones, tablets and other computing equipment. But it is not simply the hardware costs that need to be considered. The business models of many IoT companies are based on a subscription model whereby users make ongoing payments for the value-added services the products enable. In the United Kingdom, Google's Nest Cam home monitoring system comprises a Wi-Fi-enabled surveillance camera which retails for approximately £150 but also requires a monthly subscription of £8 if users want to be able to review historical video footage. As with mobile phone subscriptions it is possible that the price of IoT hardware will be subsidised by ongoing subscriptions for users. Until acceptable and easily understandable tariff schemes are developed, pricing will be an issue for domestic consumers.

Price sensitivities and priorities are different in industrial IoT settings, where demonstrable cost savings can be a spur to adoption. However, the complexities of the industrial IoT mean that installation and running costs are only one of the economic factors which need to be considered. The reconfiguration of business processes made possible by the enhanced data capture from IoT sensors and devices could have serious implications for the structures of many organisations. Those companies which can adapt their processes and build new services and revenue streams off the back of IoT initiatives will be the ones which stand to benefit the most. The issue of pricing systems, new revenue streams and innovative business models will be considered in more detail in Chapter 5.

Social barriers

Despite what many economists still think, people are not purely rational machines who make calculated purchase decisions on the basis of price and utility value. This is particularly true with many of the IoT products and services being launched into the market. Purchasers of Nest thermostats appreciate the ability to control their heating from their smartphones, but may be less happy that the thermostat can tell if anyone is in the house and, if so, which room(s) they are in. This concern may be just a general unease about sharing this information with Google or it could be for more practical reasons. Potential burglars would certainly like to know if a house is empty before they decide to break in. Although not a straightforward process, researchers have shown it is possible to hack into a Nest thermostat and take control of it (Storm, 2014).

Fitness trackers are popular devices amongst users for monitoring their activity, but as they become more sophisticated, the amount of data they collect increases. These data are usually uploaded to the cloud so users can monitor their fitness levels over time and may include levels of activity, heart rate, recovery times and dietary habits. From a privacy perspective, this is very sensitive data and needs to be secured safely. However, the security systems service providers maintain vary enormously and are subject to different legal regimes depending on where the users and servers are located. The leaking of personal data from illegal hacking is not unusual, and until trusted and secure systems are put in place, many people will be reluctant to share their health and fitness information with third parties. The issues of privacy, surveillance and possible legal and technical remedies will be considered in detail in Chapter 6, where the risks and benefits of a pervasive IoT will be weighed up.

References

Abernathy, W.J. and Utterback, J.M., 1978. Patterns of industrial innovation. *Technology Review*, 64, pp.254–228.

Baldwin, C. and Woodard, J., 2009. The architecture of platforms: A unified view. In: *Platforms, Markets and Innovation*. Ed. A. Gawer. Cheltenham: Edward Elgar, pp.19–44.

Bellini, H., Shope, B., Dunham, G., Bang, M., Moawalla, M., Cabral, M., Alam, S. and Grant, M., 2014. *Software and the IoT: Platforms, Data, and Analytics*. New York: Goldman Sachs, p.27.

Cisco, 2014. *The Internet of Everything – A $19 Trillion Opportunity*. Available at: www.cisco.com/web/services/portfolio/consulting-services/documents/consulting-services-capturing-ioe-value-aag.pdf.

Evans, P. and Annunziata, M., 2012. *Industrial Internet: Pushing the Boundaries of Minds and Machines*. Fairfield, CT: General Electric Co.

Gawer, A. and Cusumano, M.A., 2002. *Platform Leadership: How Intel, Microsoft and Cisco Drive Industry Innovation*. Boston, MA: Harvard Business School Press.

Gibbs, S., 2015. Samsung Launches SmartThings Internet of Things Hub. *The Guardian*. [online] 3 Sep. Available at: www.theguardian.com/technology/2015/sep/03/samsung-launches-smartthings-internet-of-things-hub.

Gilbert, D., 2015. Hive 2 begins Major Push by British Gas into Smart Home with Range of Connected Devices. *International Business Times*. Available at: www.ibtimes.co.uk/hive-2-begins-major-push-by-british-gas-into-smart-home-range-connected-devices-1510864.

Greenstein, S., 2009. Open platform development and the commercial internet. In: *Platforms, Markets and Innovation*. Ed. A. Gawer. Cheltenham: Edward Elgar, pp.219–248.

IDC, 2014. *IDC Market in a Minute: Internet of Things*. [online]. Available at: www.idc.com/downloads/idc_market_in_a_minute_iot_infographic.pdf.

IDC, 2015. *Smartphone OS Market Share, 2015 Q2*. [online]. Available at: www.idc.com/prodserv/smartphone-os-market-share.jsp.

IDC, 2016. *Worldwide Smartphone Growth Forecast to Slow to 3.1% in 2016*. [online]. www.idc.com. Available at: www.idc.com/getdoc.jsp?containerId=prUS41425416.

Insley, J., 2012. Car Insurance: Satellite Boxes 'Make Young Drivers Safer'. *The Guardian*. [online] 5 Apr. Available at: www.theguardian.com/money/2012/apr/05/car-insurance-premiums-telematics-satellite-box.

KPMG, 2015. *Automobile Insurance in the Era of Autonomous Vehicles*. [online]. KPMG. Available at: www.kpmg.com/us/en/issuesandinsights/articlespublications/pages/era-of-autonomous-vehicles-survey.aspx.

MarketWatch, 2015. *IBM Takes Aim at IoT with Multi Billion Investment and New Business Unit says Strategy Analytics*. [online]. Available at: www.marketwatch.com/story/ibm-takes-aim-at-iot-with-multi-billion-investment-and-new-business-unit-says-strategy-analytics-2015–08–26.

Meunier, F., Wood, A., Weiss, K., Huberty, K. and Flannery, S., 2014. *The 'Internet of Things' Is Now: Connecting the Real Economy*. Blue Papers. New York: Morgan Stanley.

NextMarket Insights, 2014. Smart Lock Market Set to See Explosive Growth in Coming Decade. *NextMarket Insights Blog*. Available at: http://nextmarket.co/blogs/news-1/12524557-smart-lock-market-set-to-see-explosive-growth-in-coming-decade.

O'Halloran, D. and Kvochko, E., 2015. *Industrial Internet of Things: Unleashing the Potential of Connected Products and Services*. Geneva: World Economic Forum.

Ovide, S. and Wakabayashi, D., 2015. Apple's Share of Smartphone Industry's Profits Soars to 92%. *Wall Street Journal*. [online] 12 Jul. Available at: www.wsj.com/articles/apples-share-of-smartphone-industrys-profits-soars-to-92–1436727458.

Parrish, K., 2015. *ZigBee, Z-Wave, Thread and WeMo: What's the Difference?* [online]. Available at: www.tomsguide.com/us/smart-home-wireless-network-primer,news-21085.html.

Rogers, E.M., 2003. *Diffusion of Innovations*. 5th rev. ed. New York: Simon & Schuster International.

Slaughter, A., Bean, G. and Mittal, A., 2015. *Connected Barrels: Transforming Oil and Gas Strategies with the Internet of Things*. Westlake, TX: Deloitte University Press.

Storm, D., 2014. Black Hat: Nest Thermostat Turned into a Smart Spy in 15 Seconds. *ComputerWorld*. Available at: www.computerworld.com/article/2476599/cybercrime-hacking/black-hat-nest-thermostat-turned-into-a-smart-spy-in-15-seconds.html.

Wilson, T.D., 2002. The nonsense of knowledge management. *Information Research*. [online]. Available at: http://informationr.net/ir/8-1/paper144.html.
Wolpin, S., 2014. *The First Cellphone Went on Sale 30 Years Ago for $4,000. Mashable*. [online]. Available at: http://mashable.com/2014/03/13/first-cellphone-on-sale/.
Zarco-Tejada, P., Hubbard, N. and Loudjani, P., 2014. *Precision Agriculture: An Opportunity for EU Farmers*. Available at: www.europarl.europa.eu/thinktank/en/document.html?reference=IPOL-AGRI_NT(2014)529049.
Zittrain, J., 2008. *The Future of the Internet*. London: Penguin Books.

4 IoT players

Introduction

Chapter 3 considered the key forces driving the development of the IoT, and this chapter explores some of the key companies and organisations behind these changes. The IoT landscape is in its early stage of development and, like most emerging sectors, is characterised by a wide range of companies, consortia and public bodies all vying to shape the way it develops. Some of these are individual companies seeking to gain a foothold either through a proprietary technology or by dominating a market segment. Some companies have banded together to form consortia so that technology standards can be established which will drive forward development and user adoption. In the public sector, there are a range of initiatives at the local and national levels which seek to exploit the potential of the IoT to deliver improved public services and/or stimulate economic activity around technology clusters. This chapter looks in detail at some of the key players across these different activities, examines where they sit on the IoT value chain and how they overlap and interact with each other.

The IoT value chain

In a business context, a value chain is the set of activities which add value to a product or service. Value chains can be observed within companies and are defined by how the firm manages its resources to create a market offering (Porter, 1985). The study of value chains can also take place within industries where the entire process of producing a good or service is examined and includes all the companies which add value along the way. In the context of the IoT, a simplified value chain is described in Figure 4.1, which breaks down the core activities which take place within the IoT and where different companies are able to add value along the way. At the core of the IoT are the 'Things' themselves whether they be sensors embedded in industrial processes, fitness trackers or smart thermostats. For data to be extracted from these things, they

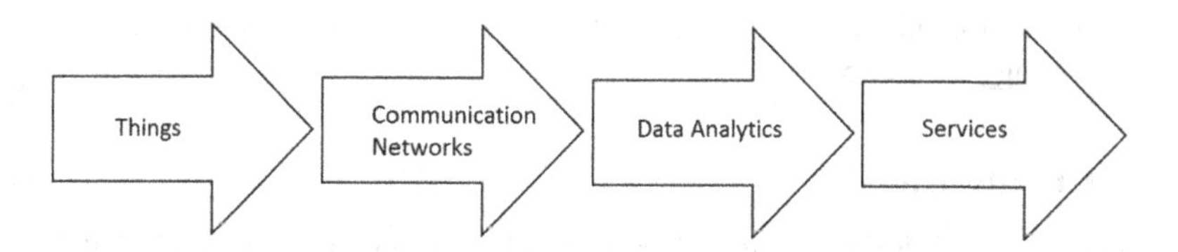

Figure 4.1 The IoT value chain

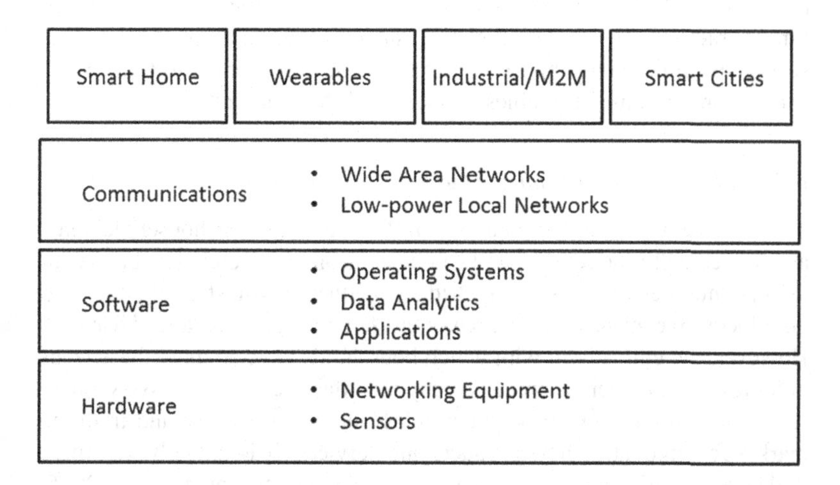

Figure 4.2 The IoT technology stack

need to be connected to a communications network, typically but not exclusively a wireless one. This data needs to then be processed within a backend system which carries out some form of analytics to make sense of what has been captured. In the final stage of this simplified model, a service is provided which uses the processed data to create value-added information which meets a market need. This could, for example, be a business information service helping a company improve its industrial processes or a historical record of fitness activity helping an athlete improve his or her training program. It is unlikely that a single company will perform all the activities on this value chain as they encompass a very broad range of business processes and require very different competencies as well as technical infrastructure.

Figure 4.2 shows the IoT technology stack and builds on the value chain to show the generic technologies powering the IoT with a selection of important end-user applications. This high-level representation of the technologies underpinning the IoT and their real-world applications informs the structure of this chapter, which looks at specific companies, consortia and public sector initiatives seeking to shape and benefit from this emerging technology landscape.

IoT hardware

At the core of the emerging IoT is the linking of the physical world to the virtual one. Information and communication (ICT) hardware, therefore, is central to the IoT's development. This can take the form of sensors, microprocessors, RFID chips and antenna, as well as complete devices such as fitness trackers, thermostats, lighting, smart meters and door locks. This section examines companies producing IoT hardware for the following categories: smart home; wearables; industrial/M2M; smart cities.

IoT hardware – smart/connected home

The dream of the so-called smart or connected home where household items are connected to the internet and can be controlled remotely has been with us for a number of years. Smart fridges, kettles, thermostats, lighting and door locks do currently exist which offer users a range of advanced features. However, the enthusiasm with which households have adopted these technologies has not been as great as many manufacturers would have wished. As we saw in the previous chapter, unless there is a real demand from the market for innovative new products and services, it is unlikely that there will be any significant take-up. It has been estimated that at the end of 2015, only 5% of US households had a smart home device and that this figure would rise to only 15% by 2021 (Economist, 2016b). There are a number of reasons for this: many appliances such as fridges and thermostats are replaced relatively infrequently; the benefits these smart devices offer are often not significant for the users and are often seen as rather frivolous; there is usually a price premium charged for smart devices which can run into the thousands of dollars for large items such as fridges; the range of different standards device manufacturers utilise when it comes to remote control and data sharing makes many customers reluctant to invest in technologies which new entrants may render obsolete; installing and getting smart devices to talk to each other can be difficult for non-technical consumers (Bradshaw, 2015).

As with other sub-sectors of the IoT, it is interesting to observe companies moving into industries in which they have not traditionally competed. This is particularly true of the smart home, where a number of companies are attempting to extend their success in the computing and internet sectors into the production of household items. In 2014, Google spent $3.2 billion buying Nest, a maker of smart thermostats, to give it a foothold in the IoT market for domestic products (Wohlsen, 2014). It followed this with the acquisition of Dropcam, which makes connected video cameras for home surveillance, for $550 million. However, the market has not expanded as quickly as Google expected with only 1.3 million Nest thermostats being sold in 2015 (Economist, 2016b). One of the reasons for the slower than expected adoption may be the initial cost of the device and the technical skills required to install it. As with many consumer-facing innovative products, there is an initial enthusiasm amongst early adopters who are prepared to overcome technical issues so they can have the latest "thing" (Rogers, 2003). However, many products fail or falter once the early adopter market segment is saturated and the manufacturers fail to persuade the broader mass of consumers that this is a product worth investing in.

Apple is another company eager to extend its reach into the home beyond the computer and smartphone. The previous chapter described its HomeKit standard which is attempting to create a platform to allow the interconnection of household devices through an Apple gateway. Like Samsung's SmartThings IoT hub, it is not clear as of late 2016 which, if any, of these platforms will meet with market success and provide a base for third parties to launch complementary products and services. Chapter 5 considers the role of such platforms in building sustainable business models for the IoT.

Case Study – Hive

Research and analysis on the smart home and the IoT often focuses on the Nest smart thermostat which is owned by Google. An interesting competitor to Nest in the United Kingdom is Hive, which is offered by utility company British Gas, a subsidiary of British global energy company Centrica. Whereas Nest is a product which was developed and launched by a company from outside the domestic energy supply sector, Hive and its associated services is an attempt by an established energy company to extend its offerings into the domestic IoT space. British Gas signalled its intent to deliver smart home products and services when it set up its Connected Home business unit in 2012. Hive emerged from this unit in 2013 and by early 2016 was in more than 300,000 homes in the United Kingdom (Carey, 2016). In 2015, British Gas paid £44 million to acquire AlertMe, the company which provides the technology platform, Honeycomb, that powers Hive (Cookson, 2015). By late 2016, the Hive product range working on the Honeycomb platform had been extended to include connected window and door sensors, lightbulbs, motion sensors and plug sockets all connected by the Hive hub and controllable from a smartphone app. British Gas is obviously serious about its move into delivering smart home products and services and, as of late 2016, is one of the leading UK operators in this space. Whether its Honeycomb IoT platform, based on the ZigBee communications protocol, becomes a de facto standard remains to be seen, but the achievement of Hive and British Gas's large customer base (approximately 11 million customers) gives it a very good chance of success. The growing range of Honeycomb-compatible products which include home security signals that the company is attempting to extend its offerings beyond just the provision of energy services.

IoT hardware – wearables

While the penetration of the IoT into the home is still struggling in 2016 to achieve a critical mass, the market for IoT-enabled wearables, including clothing, watches, fitness and health trackers, perhaps presents a more positive picture. This is partly a reflection on the wide range of companies entering this market, but also that the perceived benefits amongst consumers are often more apparent. The global market for smart wearables is expected to rise from 248 million unit sales in 2017 to 1 billion in 2020 (Meunier et al., 2014).

One of the trends driving the adoption of the wearables category is the rise in popularity of personal fitness as witnessed by growing gym memberships in many developed economies, as well as the visible spectacle of runners around city streets. Gadgets and apps to measure performance have proliferated as users seek new ways to track and improve their progress. In June 2015, the maker of a range of wearable fitness trackers, FitBit, floated on the New York Stock Exchange (NYSE) with a market valuation of more than $4 billion (CB Insights, 2015). The high valuation was driven by the phenomenal growth of the company, which had revenues of $76 million in 2012 growing to $1.9 billion in 2015, an increase of 25 times in four years. As of late 2016, the company offered eight different wearable devices capable of measuring the physical activity of the wearer. These range from the FitBit Zip aimed at children and casual users and available for approximately $50 to the Surge for serious sporting amateurs costing approximately $250. Depending on the model, the devices measure steps taken, distance covered and vital signs such as pulse and sleep patterns. What links them all is the ability for users to extract data wirelessly from the devices so that they can be analysed to track progress and compare performance with other users. Similar devices are also offered by Microsoft, Garmin, Adidas and Nike. For the manufacturers of fitness trackers, the value lies in both the revenues from product sales and the data users upload to their monitoring services. Depending on the openness of the platforms offered by the providers and format of the data produced by the devices, users can become locked in to these companies once they have built up a historical record of exercise regimes and corresponding performance. This is less likely to apply to more casual users, but those who take their exercise seriously will want to track their performance over time.

Case Study – Garmin

Garmin is an American company founded in 1989 to provide navigation systems based on Global Positioning Satellite (GPS) technology for the marine and military sectors. Since then its hardware has extended to consumer-oriented products for car navigation and handheld and wearable location trackers. While Garmin has been a market leader in portable navigation and location tracking devices for a number of years, it is being challenged in this market by a number of new entrants, including Samsung, Apple, Nike and Fitbit. GPS technology in the consumer space has become commoditised and is now a standard feature in phones and smart watches. Users, particularly amateur fitness enthusiasts, increasingly demand more than just data about where they are and how far they have run or cycled. Value-added services such as activity history, tracking friends' exercise routines and combining activity data with personal fitness metrics all accessible via the web or smartphone apps are becoming the norm. While Garmin's products are generally accepted to be of high quality, it has struggled to build an online ecosystem around them in the way that some smartphone apps such as Endomondo and Runkeeper have in the software space. As a number of competent and respected technology hardware companies are finding, the IoT is driving them to become software and service players as well. Apple and Samsung have understood this, and their smart watches combine the utility of fitness trackers with a broader platform from which other services can be delivered.

While the fitness trackers discussed previously are becoming relatively commonplace, an emerging category in the IoT wearables sector is smart clothing. By embedding sensors into the clothing itself, wearers can measure a range of vital signs as well as body size metrics without the need for carrying a separate device. The MyZone sports bra measures heart rate and transmits the data to a smartphone app via Bluetooth while Lumo Run shorts track a range of running metrics, including cadence, ground contact time and stride length. The shorts and shirts Athos produces can measure heart rate, breathing and muscle activity through the use of sensors within smart fabrics. Outside the sporting sector, the LikeAGlove smart leggings allow wearers to create an accurate picture of their lower body to help find jeans which fit their unique size. The market for smart clothing is at a very early stage and will need to overcome a number of challenges, including making clothes which can be safely put through a washing machine without damaging the sensors. However, one of the largest manufacturers of sports clothing clearly sees a future in being able to combine computing intelligence with sporting apparel. In 2015, Under Armour bought two fitness tracking apps, Endomondo and MyFitnessPal, for more than $500 million (Germano, 2015). A key driver of the acquisitions was access to the 120 million users of these two apps in the United States and across Europe to provide a platform from which to launch future ranges of smart sports clothes. As Under Armour's CEO stated in September 2015 following these deals:

> If we believe that our future is going to be defined by these [mobile wearable devices that are] hard pieces of glass or plastic that sit in our back pockets [that we know today], you're crazy. It is going to convert into apparel.
>
> (Bridgwater, 2015)

Whether Under Armour's $500 million bet will pay off is debatable, but the attraction of clothes which can monitor our vital signs is obvious both in sporting and more general health scenarios. There are both technical and business challenges which will need to be overcome before smart clothing becomes mainstream. The technical challenge of combining clothing with sensitive communications technology in a way that can stand up to the daily punishment of sporting activities and washing machines has already been mentioned. However, there is also the commercial issue of whether enough people will be prepared to pay a premium for such products which will depend on the perceived benefits. It is very likely that, if the technology can be perfected, then it will only ever appeal to athletes who are serious about tracking their performance. For students of business, one of the most interesting aspects to observe is the clash of very different industries, clothing and computing technology, as they struggle to define this emerging category. Although Under Armour would claim it uses advanced fabric technologies in its sportswear, it is essentially producing products, shirts and shorts, which have been made for centuries. Like all clothing companies, its business model has been to manufacture and then sell products for a fixed price while having little or no relationship with the end consumer. As with many consumer-facing IoT companies, including those we saw in the smart home section, this is set to change. Under Armour's purchase of Endomondo and MyFitnessPal signals an attempt to build closer relationships with its customers and move into creating more subscription-based revenue streams rather than one-off single payments for apparel. The next chapter on business models will consider this challenge in more detail.

IoT hardware – industrials/M2M

Less visible to most of us than the consumer-facing IoT of smart homes and wearables but of more economic significance is where the IoT meets the industrial landscape. Ripe for transformation by advanced computing and communications technologies, the industrial sector is investing heavily in the IoT as it looks to save costs by streamlining processes but also create new opportunities from the data generated by its activities.

The first industrial revolution which began in the United Kingdom in the eighteenth century was driven by the application of steam power to the manufacture of goods from the extraction of raw materials from the ground to the creation to the powering of factories and the railways which moved the materials and finished products around the country. Later, the use of electricity in the twentieth century alongside the building of power grids within developed economies produced even greater efficiencies which were improved through the application of more scientific management techniques. ICTs have helped industrial firms further improve their operating efficiencies but not, perhaps, as fast or as far as many forecasters predicted when computers entered the workplace (Brynjolfsson, 1993).[1] More recently, the rapid global rise and adoption of the internet as a communications platform has impacted much economic activity, but this has largely been confined to business to consumer (B2C) sectors of media and retail rather than the business to business (B2B) sectors dominated by the industrial sectors of manufacturing, logistics, building, agriculture and energy. Of the predicted $11 trillion global economic impact of the IoT by 2025, consultants McKinsey and Co. estimate the majority of this, approximately $7 trillion, will be seen in the B2B space (Manyika et al., 2015). Ritchie and colleagues (2014) call this new revolution the move from "bricks" to "bits" as data transforms industrial processes, many of which have not changed for decades. Developed economies which have built their success on the manufacturing sector, including China and Germany, see this transformation as both an opportunity and a threat and have put in place national strategies to help companies with the transition. In Germany, they call it "Industrie 4.0", and the Chinese have set in place a national program they are calling "made in China 2025" (O'Halloran and Kvochko, 2015).

Many of the hardware players playing a significant part in the industrial/M2M sectors of the IoT are large, established companies, including Rockwell, Siemens, ABB, Hitachi, Cisco, Schneider Electric and Mitsubishi. They already have the experience of working with industrial partners on large projects and understand the dynamics of applying complex, industrial solutions at scale. It is rare for a single company to be able to supply all the components for large industrial IoT projects as the range of technologies involved is often very broad. Within the manufacturing sector, for example, Cisco works with Rockwell Automation to offer what they call a "Connected Factory Solution" which plays to Cisco's strengths in communications hardware and Rockwell's experience in control systems which combine sensors with computing infrastructure. At the heart of the application of the IoT to the factory floor is the more efficient management of all the inputs to the production process, as well as the equipment on the assembly line. Typically, these solutions allow the tracking in real time of components on assembly lines, monitor production equipment for faults and manage the despatch of factory outputs from the factory gate to the customer. As outlined in the following section on the software players in the industrial IoT space, a number of hardware suppliers are becoming software and services providers. Trumpf, for example, a German company which makes metalworking equipment for manufacturers, has developed an online service called Axoom which connect its machines to a backend network that can predict when a machine will need a spare part (Economist, 2015).

Case Study – *Würth* Industrie Service GmbH & Co.

Würth Industrie Service is a subsidiary of the German *Würth* Group and was founded in 1999. It supplies a range of industrial equipment for factories with a focus on the automobile industry. It is at the forefront of factory automation solutions and offers a production line component supply system it calls RFID Kanban. One of its products in this line is the iBin launched in 2013 and which uses optical, RFID and wireless technology to automatically detect when components in containers on a production line are running low. When a container of components reaches a pre-determined level, an automatic order is placed to the supplier for a new delivery. This system also allows factory managers to perform an inventory stock take in seconds by amalgamating the data from the iBins in use. It has been estimated that the use of such automated systems could save as much as 20% to 50% of factory inventory-carrying costs (Manyika et al., 2015).

Agriculture is another sector which stands to benefit from the application of IoT technologies. While there are economic benefits to the development of IoT systems for the manufacturing sector, the importance of the IoT to farmers is even greater. The global population is forecast to rise from 7.3 billion in 2015 to 9.7 billion by 2050 (United Nations, 2015). At a time when the pressures on farmers to produce enough food are already intense and much of the world's viable farmland is already under cultivation, the application of new technologies will be crucial if everyone is to be fed. As well as the production of improved crop varieties and less consumption of meat, a vital part of the solution will be the more efficient use of existing farmland. IoT technologies in the form of soil sensors, equipment monitoring and drones are already being used in developed and developing economies to this end. This is often referred to as 'precision agriculture' and is: "a whole-farm management approach using information technology, satellite positioning (GNSS) data, remote sensing and proximal data gathering" (Zarco-Tejada, Hubbard and Loudjani, 2014). Having access to real-time data on soil moisture and chemical composition as well as satellite or drone imagery of crop health allows farmers to far more accurately target water and fertiliser to specific areas of fields which need it most while not wasting it on areas which do not need attention.

Farms have been using satellite imagery and images taken by planes for a number of years, but this has been expensive and the pictures are often out of date by the time they reach the farmer. The rise of drones fitted with high-definition cameras, GPS, radio communications modules and infrared sensors now allows farmers to monitor crop health across thousands of acres far more cheaply and accurately than was previously possible. Paying for a light aircraft to photograph aerial views of a farm with precision equipment can cost up to $1,000 an hour, while a drone with the necessary equipment can be bought off the shelf from companies such as DIY Drones for $1,000 outright (Anderson, 2015). Because the drones fly just a few metres above ground level, can utilise infrared cameras and create images over a time series, crop health, pest infestations and growth rates can be accurately tracked.

The world's largest manufacturer of agricultural equipment, John Deere, has been fitting its tractors with GPS sensors since 2001. By tracking the movements of their GPS-equipped tractors, farmers can ensure they have not missed parts of fields or gone over the same place twice when planting or fertilising. When planting, individual seeds can be placed with an accuracy of 3 cm and at harvest time the rate at which crops are pulled or cut from the ground can be measured (Economist, 2016b). Over time this allows the farmer to produce yield maps of fields, which helps with planning the following year's planting and crop rotation. Unmanned farm equipment is slowly starting to appear and is, perhaps, a natural evolution of the tractor. Emerging from the research laboratories of the University of Sydney's Australian Centre for Field Robotics is the Robot for Intelligent Perception and Precision Application (RIPPA) (University of Sydney, 2015). This autonomous, solar-powered vehicle is equipped with sensors on its underside and can follow a precise path between rows of crops, monitoring the health of individual plants and delivering herbicides and fertiliser to those which need it most.

Similar to John Deere's addition of smart sensors and communications equipment to its farm machinery is Caterpillar's use of IoT technologies to improve the monitoring of its heavy industrial and construction equipment, an initiative the company calls "the internet of big things". By early 2016, more than 400,000 pieces of Caterpillar equipment had connectivity built into them with the company building this into all its products by mid-2016 (du Preez, 2016). The advantage for users of this equipment is the ability to track wear and tear of individual machine components and predict when parts will need replacing before they break and lead to more expensive repair problems. The advantages of this are particularly apparent to customers such as mining companies which operate fleets of unmanned Caterpillar mining trucks that run 24 hours a day and carry up to 240-ton payloads. Being able to remotely measure oil pressure, fuel levels and tyre pressures, amongst other variables, can increase operating efficiencies by up to 40% (Maidenberg, 2015).

More directly relevant to most people is the use of IoT hardware within the buildings many of us work in. It has been estimated that approximately 20% of all energy in the United States is consumed by commercial buildings on heating, ventilation, lighting and air conditioning (Kwatra and Essig, 2014). Much of this energy is wasted through the lighting and heating of empty rooms as well as the inefficient maintenance of existing systems. Building management systems (BMS) which monitor environmental conditions within buildings via sensors have been deployed for a number of years, but their proprietary nature and the inability of many of them to interface with other information systems has restricted their potential. A more integrated approach using open protocols could change this and is being promoted by large technology vendors such as Cisco. At one of its test-bed deployments in the United Kingdom, Cisco, in conjunction with Johnson Controls, has used the Open Building Information Exchange (oBIX) protocol to link lighting and heating sensors and controls with the building's communications network so that all the environmental variables can be monitored. It is estimated that for a typical 13,000 m2 building such as the one being tested, energy cost savings of approximately £120,000 per year could be made (Smith, 2015). The environmental benefits of such deployments, if they can be replicated across the mass of commercial office space, are obvious apart from the financial benefits to tenants.

Before energy enters a building, it has to pass through the gas or electric network which provides its power. Energy as well as water utility companies are one of the largest users of remote sensors across their networks and are investing heavily in IoT technologies to raise efficiencies. In Australia, for example, water leaks cost the providers $1.4 billion to fix each year (Tata, 2015). By applying smart sensors to allow preventive maintenance rather than simply responding to leaks as they occur, it is estimated that approximately 20% of these costs could be saved (Bajkowski, 2015). The development of so-called smart grids where the combination of smart meters in homes and commercial premises allows energy providers to monitor in real time how much energy is being used at the building level promises to increase energy efficiency. As more devices in the home become connected as part of a broad IoT network, it will be possible for utility companies to switch them on and off at times of electricity generation surplus or deficit. Domestic customers, for example, could leave a washing machine loaded with dirty clothes waiting for it to be switched on automatically by their energy provider when electricity prices are at their lowest under a variable pricing scenario (Accenture, 2015).

Case Study – Varentec

As more households and commercial buildings install solar panels on their roofs, the management of electric power grids becomes more complicated. Multiple sources of power generation and an intermittent supply of solar energy due to cloud cover places burdens on the grid in terms of balancing the central supply with variances in demand throughout the day. Varentec, a US company, offers a range of products and services to help electricity supply companies manage their grids more efficiently under these scenarios. By placing its networked ENGO devices at strategic points across a power grid, the company can monitor the supply and demand levels and inject power into the network as needed. It has been estimated that this can lead to 5% savings for power companies, which is up to five times more than traditional solutions for managing supply levels (John, 2016). The networked nature of this solution allows this process to be automated, removing the need for manual interventions. The potential for solutions such as Varentec's when combined with smart meters in buildings and the remote control of electrical devices in the home and workplace alongside distributed power generation and storage, promises to revolutionise energy generation and use.

IoT hardware – smart cities

One of the defining characteristics of the nineteenth and twentieth centuries was the mass migration of people from the countryside to cities. This has continued in the current century and is particularly marked in developing economies such as India, China and Nigeria. Between 1990 and 2014, Delhi, India's capital city, doubled its population from 12 million to 24 million (Sengupta, 2014). In 2015, more than half of the world's population lived in towns and cities, and by 2030 this is expected to rise to two thirds (UNFPA, 2015). The combination of rising town and city populations and the increased density of dwellings, places enormous pressures on essential services such as transport, utilities, health and education. Many see the IoT as a way to increase the efficiency with which these services are delivered and improve the quality of living of city dwellers. Part of this involves the development and take-up of IoT technologies and services at the domestic and industrial levels which were considered in previous sections. However, there is also an important role for town planners as well as local and national governments if 'smart cities' are to become a reality.

In the United Kingdom, a joint venture between Bristol City Council and the University of Bristol has fitted 1,500 lampposts with sensors as part of a broader initiative to produce open data sets about conditions within the city (Economist, 2016a). Being able to measure air quality from 1,500 sensors around the city should produce a much richer picture of environmental conditions than the five monitoring stations the city council has operated since 1994 (Bristol City Council, 2016). Air quality within towns and cities is becoming an increasing concern, particularly with the rise in popularity of diesel cars. In the United Kingdom, it has been estimated that long-term exposure to air pollution is causing approximately 29,000 premature deaths a year (Public Health England, 2014). While air sensors themselves cannot prevent pollution, they can raise levels of awareness, putting pressure on public bodies to tackle the problem and, when the data is particularly granular as in Bristol, allow individuals to avoid certain areas.

In Abu Dhabi, an 'adaptive traffic control' system has been implemented through an upgrade of the traffic lights and the installation of traffic sensors at 125 intersections in the city. The sensors can monitor traffic flows and identify specific types of vehicles. These data are fed through to the traffic lights, which gives priority to emergency vehicles and buses and, if a bus is running more than five minutes late, will give priority to that vehicle at the lights. It is estimated this has increased traffic flow by up to 25%, reduces pollution and, if rolled out globally, could be worth more than $500 billion in terms of costs savings to local economies (Manyika et al., 2015).

Case Study – Telensa

Telensa is a UK-based company founded in 2005 which uses wireless technologies to help local authorities more efficiently manage municipal lighting and parking. The company utilises Ultra-Narrow-Band (UNB) technology in the nodes it attaches to streetlights, allowing the remote management of the lighting so they can be dimmed at certain times of the day and even switched on if a crime is reported to police in specific areas. By early 2016, 700,000 of the 7 million streetlights in the United Kingdom had been fitted with Telensa nodes which cost approximately £45 each. An installation of 33,000 in Doncaster, UK, in 2015 is estimated to save the local council £1.3 million a year in energy and maintenance costs (Hickey, 2016). Telensa's smart parking solution places magnetic strips on parking bays which are activated by cars parking on them. This sends a signal to the Telensa network and electronic street signs then direct drivers to free spaces. The Telensa nodes can also be used to send data about other environmental conditions such as air quality and road driving conditions.

IoT software

While it is the IoT hardware which is usually most visible, particularly when it comes to our homes and the devices we wear and carry with us, the software which powers them is generally more significant from a business perspective. Much of the hardware underpinning the IoT has become commoditised to the extent that it is built to a price and is often hidden from the consumer's eye. While we probably know the brand of our smartphone or tablet PC, it is unlikely many of us know the manufacturer of the processors and sensors they contain. The history of the personal computer since the 1980s and the smartphone since 2007 has been dominated by the creators of the software which runs on them. One generally buys either a Microsoft Windows PC or a Mac when choosing a PC. When choosing a smartphone, we are either iPhone or Android people as it is the operating system and how vested we are in that which is often more important than the physical device itself. According to IDC (2016), of the approximately 1.5 billion smartphones sold around the world in 2016, 84% were Android and 15% were iOS (the iPhone operating system). The IoT is a far more diverse set of technologies and applications that the relatively homogenised smartphone marketplace and, for the most part, dominant software standards have not emerged. It is unlikely that one or two operating systems will predominate across the entire IoT but that certain sub-sectors such as the smart home, wearables, smart car and so forth will coalesce around a small number of software platforms. It is important to note that software in the context of the IoT is not restricted to the software behind the operating system of the 'things' themselves, but extends to the applications which manage the communications with other 'things' and hubs, the middleware which links to other applications as well as the software powering the backend data capture and analytics. According to Bellini and colleagues (2014), dominant software platforms for the industrial/M2M sector will not emerge until the early to mid-2020s, but the consumer-facing IoT will reach this point much sooner. Morrish (2013) agrees that no single software solution exists for the industrial IoT but that some companies such as Bosch, SAP and ThingWorx are making progress in creating platforms which show promise in tackling specific software issues.

IoT software – smart/connected home

Attempts to create software platforms for the smart home are being undertaken by some of the world's largest technology companies and these were briefly discussed in Chapter 3. Despite large investments in product development and marketing by Google, Apple, Amazon and Samsung, amongst others, no software platform has been able to replicate what has happened in the smartphone sector. Of course this may change as third-party hardware developers possibly migrate to one system as it gains critical mass. If this happens, then we may see a virtuous circle of economic success for the winners and a vicious circle of decline for the losers. In 2016, for example, it would be a brave/foolish developer who built their smartphone app solely for Windows or Blackberry. It is also possible that no software platforms dominate within the smart home and it remains a fragmented array of products and applications each delivering specific services such as door locks, video monitoring and temperature and lighting control. Some commentators see the rush to create software platforms for the home as a mistake and argue that companies should focus on providing solutions which address real consumer needs. Wolf (2016) cites Skybell and Ring as companies which have been successful in the smart home market because they have not tried to create a platform but rather a video doorbell solution which users actually understand and want. While specific solutions such as these may be successful in the short to medium term, the history of computing technologies indicates that the market will eventually grow around integrated platforms (Gawer and Cusumano, 2002, 2014).

From a business perspective, companies are adopting a variety of approaches with respect to developing software for the IoT. Google is adopting a similar approach with its Brillo operating system (OS) as it did, very successfully, with Android by making it open source. This, in theory at least, encourages other hardware and software developers to build products and services on a platform which is not proprietary to a particular company. However, while the operating system itself may be open source and, therefore, open to modification, there are ways in which Google can control the direction and ways its OS is used. Within Android, for example, Google is able to lay down rules for handset manufacturers if they wish to provide access to the Google Play app store. These rules include forcing manufacturers to include a number of Google apps on the phones, including Google Search and the Chrome browser. Similar to Microsoft's legal problems over bundling the Internet Explorer web browser with Windows in the 1990s, in 2016, the European Commission (EC) of the European Union (EU) filed a formal antitrust charge against Google with respect to Android rules for handset makers (Charlton, 2016). It is possible that developers of smart home solutions may be reluctant to commit to Google's Brillo OS if they perceive similar restrictions will apply to them further down the line. While open source software offers a number of advantages in terms of flexibility for developers, there are also advantages with more proprietary solutions in terms of stability and consistency. Glasskeys (2015) sums up the dilemma facing developers in the smart home sector:

> For many developers and users, the decision to use free/open source (FOSS) software is highly personal in nature, based on moral and philosophical grounds. This means Google's scheme of pulling a long-term 'bait-and-switch' on these users deserves extra condemnation. And while history has revealed the full imperfection of Google's competitors, developers writing apps for Apple and Microsoft OSes know from the start that iOS and Windows are closed source, and are likely to remain that way forever.
>
> (Glasskeys, 2015)

Similar to its approach with the iPhone, Apple is adopting a more tightly controlled smart home software framework, HomeKit. Manufacturers of devices which want them to be accessible and controllable via iOS phones must be certified by Apple, a process which can be complicated and, in some cases, has required third parties to modify the microprocessors running within their products. As with the iPhone, the trade-off for Apple is a potentially smaller market share, but the ability to better control the security and user experience for purchasers of HomeKit-certified products and, as a consequence, charge a market premium. As we saw in Chapter 3, this strategy has been very profitable for Apple with the vast majority of profits within the smartphone hardware market going to the company despite its relatively small market share. However, if HomeKit devices are going to be made by third-party developers, then Apple will not reap the profits from their sales. Apple's strategy with HomeKit is focused on driving new sales and locking existing customers into the iPhone and iPad as only those devices are able to operate HomeKit equipment.

Case Study – Amazon

How the large technology companies such as Google, Apple and Samsung are approaching their development of products and services for the smart home is indicative of their core business models. Google is a software company which seeks to gather and extract value from customer information, and this is reflected in its focus on developing operating systems for home devices. Apple is essentially a hardware company and sees the smart home as a way to drive sales of its iPhone and iPad. Samsung makes consumer goods and is busy trying to integrate smart features into its domestic products such as fridges and televisions. Amazon is an online retail company which has used its Kindle Fire tablets as well as its streaming video and music services to attract and retain its online shoppers. Its smart home efforts are focused around a device called the Amazon Echo launched in the United States in 2015. This is a cylindrical object approximately 24 cm tall which contains a speaker and seven microphones. It is designed to respond to voice commands and can stream music, perform web searches and order goods from the Amazon online store. It can also be linked to smart home devices from third-party providers so users can instruct the Echo to dim the lights, change the temperature or turn other devices on or off. Amazon allows developers to create what it calls "recipes" which can link to a variety of online services allowing, for example, pizzas and Uber taxis to be ordered simply by talking to the Echo.

IoT software – data analytics

While domestic consumers will generally buy IoT products to make their lives easier by automating routine tasks such as controlling the heating, opening doors or managing lighting, industrial users are much more focused on the data generated by the IoT. Making sense of these data to improve business processes and decision making requires often complex backend systems to store and analyse these outputs.

Traditional software for managing databases within organisations is often not appropriate for many of the much larger data sets being generated by large-scale IoT implementations. New ways of managing so called Big Data have been developed by some of the large internet companies, including Google, Facebook and Amazon. Database software solutions built around, for example, Hadoop and NoSQL frameworks, have proven themselves capable of handling massive volumes of data at very high speed. Companies offering data storage and analytics solutions built on these technologies include Microsoft with its Azure platform, GE with its Predix platform and Amazon with its Web Services (AWS). Each of these companies has developed offerings for IoT developers.

Once the data from a large-scale IoT implementation have been captured and processed within one of the data platforms such as those listed earlier, the analysis and visualisation of the information is crucial if any meaningful decisions are to be made on the back of it. Effective data visualisation is where the value can be realised from the 'digital oil' being extracted from the IoT. Business intelligence (BI) systems are nothing new, but increasing value is being placed on the currency of the information being presented. Historical reporting of business activities is still important, but a greater competitive advantage can be attained by organisations able to act more quickly on data as it is being generated. Companies offering enhanced data visualisation and reporting services are established BI players such as SAP but also newer entrants including Splunk and Tableau.

Case Study – GE Predix

General Electric's (GE) Predix is a cloud-based service for industrial customers to help them make sense of their IoT data and extract value from it. GE describes Predix as a platform-as-a-service (PAAS) offering which is focused on the specific needs of industrial customers. The applications developed on the Predix platform include managing the data from oil rigs and tracking in real time the data outputs from jet engines while they are in the air. Predix generated almost $6 billion in revenue for GE in 2015, and the company expects it will be handling data from 50 million devices by 2020 (Gillin, 2016). In 2016, the Predix platform was used to manage and analyse data from an active volcano in Nicaragua from 80 sensors which had been placed within the erupting mountain. An objective of this project was to make the data available publicly online via the platform to allow anyone to use the Predix tools to better understand the dynamics of volcanic eruptions. GE's large investments in Predix marks its move to being a service as well as a product company.

IoT communications

The previous sections in this chapter have looked at IoT hardware and the software running on these devices. This section examines the connectivity technologies, standards and protocols which put the 'internet' in the IoT. Connectivity is obviously an essential element of any IoT installation as it allows both user control of the 'things' and data to be extracted and remotely managed.

As with the hardware and software layers of the IoT, there are various companies, organisations and consortia trying to develop and impose standards to allow interoperability between devices and systems. Some of the communication technologies used within the IoT are already widely used, including Bluetooth, Wi-Fi and GSM. Others, such as WeMo, ZigBee and Thread, are used by IoT device manufacturers but have not clearly achieved a sustainable position in the market. Finally, there are communication standards, particularly around 5G, which are still, in 2016, under discussion and development and have not yet been launched.

Some companies have made very profitable businesses from developing software and dominating specific applications such as Windows with desktop operating systems and Oracle with large database systems. Others such as Apple have derived massive profits by selling differentiated hardware which consumers are prepared to pay a premium for. However, it is unusual for a company to be able to make money directly from ownership of a communications standard. Wi-Fi and Bluetooth are managed and licensed by non-profit organisations which ensure these technologies are developed and used in accordance with a strict set of principles ensuring a stable and reliable protocol for third parties to build devices incorporating them. This generally operates in the long-term interests of the broader technology landscape which benefits from robust and common standards that make hardware interoperable. Competing and conflicting standards make hardware and software more difficult and can be off-putting to consumers who demand simplicity and devices which can communicate with each other.

As we have seen in the previous sections, the IoT is a very broad set of applications and technologies, and there is not likely to be a single communications protocol/standard which will meet all needs. Some devices require communication chips which consume very little power and only need to operate over short distances, while others may be less restricted in their power requirements but have to transmit data over many miles. A common link between most of these systems is the requirement for standardisation, which is where non-profit bodies such as the Wi-Fi Alliance and the Bluetooth Special Interest Group play important roles. Fifth-generation (5G) mobile network services which are expected to be rolled out from 2020 are being developed by the Next Generation Mobile Networks (NGMN)

Alliance formed in 2006 by mobile network operators and handset manufacturers. As well as specifying the characteristics for even faster mobile networks than the current 4G standard, the NGMN Alliance is also factoring in the requirements for the IoT as the network operators see this as an important future revenue stream and don't wish to be side-lined by competing technologies for data transmission.

Note

1 This has been referred to as the 'productivity paradox' which Erik Brynjolfsson developed in the early 1990s. He analysed the apparent discrepancy between the rapid rise in the power of computers and the much slower increases in efficiencies within firms and industries which were investing in computing technologies.

References

Accenture, 2015. *The New Energy Consumer*. Available at: www.accenture.com/us-en/insight-new-energy-consumer-architecting-future.

Anderson, C., 2015. How Drones Came to Your Local Farm. *MIT Technology Review*. [online]. Available at: www.technologyreview.com/s/526491/agricultural-drones/.

Bajkowski, J., 2015. Turnbull Connects Greenhouse Gasses to Internet-of-Things. *Government News*. Available at: www.governmentnews.com.au/2015/03/turnbull-connects-greenhouse-gasses-to-internet-of-things/.

Bellini, H., Shope, B., Dunham, G., Bang, M., Moawalla, M., Cabral, M., Alam, S. and Grant, M., 2014. *Software and the IoT: Platforms, Data, and Analytics*. New York: Goldman Sachs, p.27.

Bradshaw, T., 2015. The Smart Home Is Still Too Clever for Its Own Good. *Financial Times*. [online] 22 Oct. Available at: www.ft.com/cms/s/0/f9a260f4–743a-11e5-a129–3fcc4f641d98.html?siteedition=uk#axzz4469NG0Qj.

Bridgwater, A., 2015. Under Armour's New Workout – Here Comes the Internet of (Apparel) Things. *Forbes*. [online]. Available at: www.forbes.com/sites/adrianbridgwater/2015/09/23/under-armours-new-workout-here-comes-the-internet-of-apparel-things/.

Bristol City Council, 2016. *Bristol City Council Air Quality Monitoring*. [online]. Available at: www.bristol.airqualitydata.com/.

Brynjolfsson, E., 1993. The productivity paradox of information technology. *Communications of the ACM*, 36(12), pp.66–77.

Carey, S., 2016. How British Gas Is Moving Beyond Hive and Managing an 'Explosion' of IoT Data Using Open-Source Tech. *ComputerworldUK*. [online]. Available at: www.computerworlduk.com/data/how-british-gas-is-managing-explosion-of-iot-data-with-apache-technology-3638798/.

CB Insights, 2015. *Analyzing the Internet of Things Investment Landscape*. New York: CB Insights.

Charlton, A., 2016. Google Slammed by EU for 'Stifling Competition and Restricting Innovation' with Android Rules. *International Business Times UK*. [online]. Available at: www.ibtimes.co.uk/google-charged-by-eu-imposing-abusive-anti-competitive-rules-android-manufacturers-1555783.

Cookson, R., 2015. British Gas Buys 'Smart Home' Tech Company AlertMe. *Financial Times*. [online] 13 Feb. Available at: www.ft.com/cms/s/0/16c90ea4-b38d-11e4-a45f-00144feab7de.html.

Economist, 2015. Does Deutschland Do Digital? *The Economist*, 21 Nov., pp.67–69.

Economist, 2016a. Data Deluge. *The Economist*, 19 Mar., p.26.

Economist, 2016b. Where the Smart Is. *The Economist*, 11 Jun., pp.65–66.

Gawer, A. and Cusumano, M.A., 2002. *Platform Leadership: How Intel, Microsoft and Cisco Drive Industry Innovation*. Boston, MA: Harvard Business School Press.

Gawer, A. and Cusumano, M.A., 2014. Industry platforms and ecosystem innovation. *Journal of Product Innovation Management*, 31(3), pp.417–433.

Germano, S., 2015. Under Armour Acquires MyFitnessPal for $475 Million. *Wall Street Journal*. [online] 4 Feb. Available at: www.wsj.com/articles/under-armour-to-acquire-myfitnesspal-for-475-million-1423086478.

Gillin, P., 2016. How GE Predix Tackles the Unique Challenges of the Industrial IoT. *SiliconANGLE*. Available at: http://siliconangle.com/blog/2016/08/15/how-ge-predix-tackles-the-unique-challenges-of-the-industrial-iot/.

Glasskeys, S., 2015. 3 Reasons IoT Developers Should Steer Clear of Brillo OS. *ITworld*. [online]. Available at: www.itworld.com/article/2938527/operating-systems/three-reasons-iot-developers-should-steer-clear-of-brillo-os.html.

Hickey, S., 2016. The Innovators: The Smart Systems Driving Motorists towards Smarter Cities. *The Guardian*. [online] 3 Apr. Available at: www.theguardian.com/business/2016/apr/03/the-innovators-the-smart-systems-driving-motorists-towards-smarter-cities.

IDC, 2016. *Worldwide Smartphone Growth Forecast to Slow to 3.1% in 2016*. [online]. www.idc.com. Available at: www.idc.com/getdoc.jsp?containerId=prUS41425416.

John, J.S., 2016. *Varentec Raises $13M to Bring Grid Edge Volt/VAR Platform to Market*. [online]. Available at: www.greentechmedia.com/articles/read/varentec-raises-13m-to-bring-grid-edge-volt-var-platform-to-market.

Kwatra, S. and Essig, C., 2014. *The Promise and the Potential of Comprehensive Commercial Building Retrofit Programs*. [online]. Washington, DC: American Council for an Energy Efficient Economy. Available at: http://aceee.org/research-report/a1402.

Maidenberg, M., 2015. *Why Caterpillar Is Letting Its Geek Flag Fly*. [online]. Crain's Chicago Business. Available at: www.chicagobusiness.com/article/20150704/ISSUE01/307049995/why-caterpillar-is-letting-its-geek-flag-fly.

Manyika, J., Chui, M., Bisson, P., Woetzel, J., Dobbs, R., Bughin, J. and Aharon, D., 2015. *The Internet of Things: Mapping the Value beyond the Hype*. San Francisco, CA: McKinsey & Company.

Meunier, F., Wood, A., Weiss, K., Huberty, K. and Flannery, S., 2014. *The 'Internet of Things' Is Now: Connecting the Real Economy*. Blue Papers. New York: Morgan Stanley.

Morrish, J., 2013. The Emergence of M2M/IoT Application Platforms. *Machina Research*. [online]. Available at: www.bosch-si.com/newsroom/information-materials/analyst-reports/machina-research.html .

O'Halloran, D. and Kvochko, E., 2015. *Industrial Internet of Things: Unleashing the Potential of Connected Products and Services*. Geneva: World Economic Forum.

Porter, M.E., 1985. *Competitive Advantage: Creating and Sustaining Superior Performance*. New York: Free Press.

du Preez, D., 2016. Caterpillar CEO – 'We Have to Lead Digital. By the Summer Every Machine Will Be Connected.' *diginomica*. [online]. Available at: http://

diginomica.com/2016/04/25/caterpillar-ceo-we-have-to-lead-digital-by-the-summer-every-machine-will-be-connected/.

Public Health England, 2014. *Estimates of Mortality in Local Authority Areas Associated with Air Pollution.* [online]. Available at: www.gov.uk/government/news/estimates-of-mortality-in-local-authority-areas-associated-with-air-pollution.

Ritchie, J., Costa, D., Eisner, S.H., Matsuhashi, I. and Chow, E., 2014. *The Next Industrial Revolution: Moving from B-R-I-C-K-S to B-I-T-S. The Internet of Things.* Goldman Sachs.

Rogers, E.M., 2003. *Diffusion of Innovations*. 5th rev. ed. New York: Simon & Schuster International.

Sengupta, S., 2014. U.N. Finds Most People Now Live in Cities. *The New York Times*. [online] 10 Jul. Available at: www.nytimes.com/2014/07/11/world/more-than-half-the-global-population-growth-is-urban-united-nations-report-finds.html.

Smith, A., 2015. Giant Strides. *CIBSE Journal*, Dec., pp.44–45.

Tata, 2015. *Internet of Things: The Complete Reimaginative Force*. Mumbai, India: Tata Consultancy Services.

UNFPA, 2015. Urbanization. *UNFPA – United Nations Population Fund.* [online]. Available at: www.unfpa.org/urbanization.

United Nations, 2015. *World Population Projected to Reach 9.7 Billion by 2050.* [online]. New York: United Nations Department of Economic and Social Affairs. Available at: www.un.org/en/development/desa/news/population/2015-report.html.

University of Sydney, 2015. *RIPPA Robot Takes Farms Forward to the Future.* [online]. The University of Sydney, Engineering & Information Technologies. Available at: http://sydney.edu.au/engineering/industry/ignite/sample.shtml.

Wohlsen, M., 2014. *What Google Really Gets Out of Buying Nest for $3.2 Billion.* [online]. *WIRED*. Available at: www.wired.com/2014/01/googles-3-billion-nest-buy-finally-make-internet-things-real-us/.

Wolf, M., 2016. For Smart Home Startups, It's No Longer about Platforms, but Simplicity. *Forbes.* [online]. Available at: www.forbes.com/sites/michaelwolf/2016/05/24/for-smart-home-startups-its-no-longer-about-platforms-but-simplicity/.

Zarco-Tejada, P., Hubbard, N. and Loudjani, P., 2014. *Precision Agriculture: An Opportunity for EU Farmers*. Available at: www.europarl.europa.eu/thinktank/en/document.html?reference=IPOL-AGRI_NT(2014)529049.

5 IoT business models

Introduction

The previous chapter examined a range of companies which are developing products and services for the IoT across some of the key sectors being affected by this emerging technology. Different parts of the IoT technology stack were considered in terms of how companies fit into the broader value chain of activities which underpin the IoT. This chapter analyses in detail the ways that companies are configuring their operations to profit from the IoT by looking at the business models they are deploying. As will be seen, the IoT presents a number of opportunities as well as threats to business model design for companies as value chains in a number of industries are disrupted by the data flowing from the 'things'.

What are business models?

The study of business models is still evolving, and researchers in this field (Kiel, Arnold, Collisi and Voigt, 2016) have proposed a number of different definitions. However, the common link between most definitions is the idea that a business model defines the way a business configures it operations to deliver value for its customers and, as a consequence, create revenues and profits. Teece (2010) provides a succinct definition of the term which fits well with how most commentators approach the subject:

> The essence of a business model is in defining the manner by which the enterprise delivers value to customers, entices customers to pay for value, and converts those payments to profit. It thus reflects management's hypothesis about what customers want, how they want it, and how the enterprise can organize to best meet those needs, get paid for doing so, and make a profit.
>
> (Teece, 2010, p.172)

Although perhaps seeming rather obvious in its breakdown of firm activities, the business model concept allows the manager to segment a firm's activities and, if appropriate, reconfigure them to suit changing markets and technologies. Osterwalder and Pigneur (2010) have taken this idea and created what they call the Business Model Canvas, which is a tool for analysing, describing and designing business models. The Business Model Canvas expands Teece's definition of a business model and breaks the activities of the firm into nine segments from defining customer needs, the firm's value proposition in response to those needs, revenue streams and cost structures. Figure 5.1 shows these nine key elements of the Business Model Canvas.

Bucherer and Uckelmann (2011) argue that using the business model as a unit of analysis is an evolution from the use of value chains, popular in the 1990s. They claim that technological advances and more complex industry structures require a more nuanced approach which the business model allows. In the context of the IoT, the two authors believe new types of business models will be required, especially as information often becomes the core value proposition for companies developing products and services in this sector. In their extensive review of business models, Bucherer, Eisert and Gassmann (2012) condense Osterwalder and Pigneur's nine elements into four: value proposition, operational model,

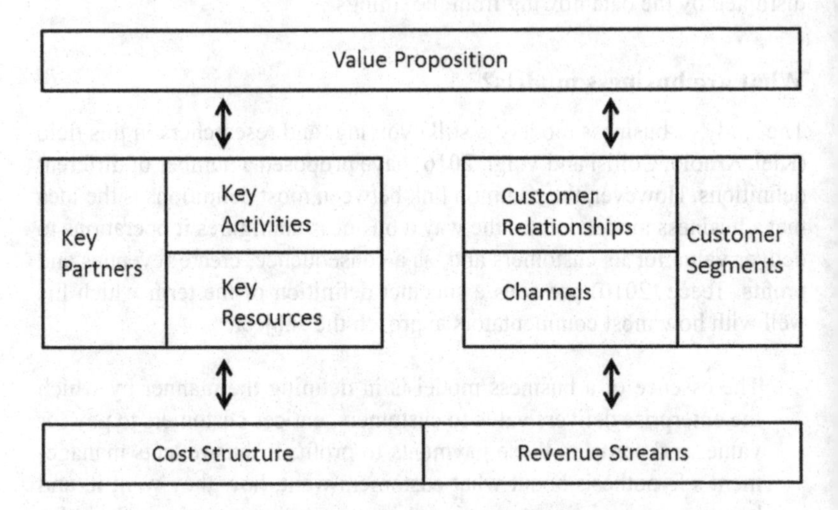

Figure 5.1 The Business Model Canvas (adapted from Osterwalder and Pigneur (2010))

financial model and customer relations. Building on this review and combining it with analysis of their own, Fleisch, Weinberger and Wortmann (2015) show the role that new information technologies, particularly the internet, have played in business model innovation since the early 1990s. They break down the role of the internet in this process into three stages:

- Web 1.0 from 1995 to 2000. During this phase, the web itself was an enabler which allowed companies to engage in ecommerce and the digitisation of previously analogue content.
- Web 2.0 from 2005 to 2015. Companies leveraged the power of social media and user-generated content to create value. Facebook and YouTube are good examples of companies which managed to harness the contributions of users to a network to create valuable platforms for advertising.
- Web 3.0 from 2015 onwards. This period, the authors argue, will see the rise of the IoT where the physical world meets the digital one and distributed sensors will create value from the information services they generate.

The key difference between the Web 2.0 and the Web 3.0 eras will be the incorporation of physical objects into the virtual world of the internet. The main business transformations we have seen so far since the rise of the internet have been focused on information industries which are better suited to digitisation than industries rooted in the manufacture of goods such as the automobile and consumer goods sectors. Fleisch, Weinberger and Wortmann (2015) use the example of the light bulb to show how an everyday object which has been used for more than 100 years can be impacted by the IoT. Until the rise of smart LED lighting, the light bulb has been a technology to light a room when switched on by a user. By adding sensors and communication capabilities the light bulb is now able to turn itself on when it detects someone entering a room and when light levels are low, can turn itself off when the person leaves the room, can adjust its brightness depending on light levels, can be configured to suit different moods of the user and can act as a burglar alarm by detecting intruders and deter burglars by flashing brightly when this happens. The light bulb can also provide historical information about the usage of rooms in commercial buildings, helping building service managers predict and optimise heating and lighting energy requirements. From a business model perspective, this creates new revenue opportunities for the light bulb manufacturers as they are able to offer additional value-added services to their customers beyond just the sale of the bulb itself.

From product to service innovation

Although the study of innovation has come to the fore in recent years as developed economies struggle to grow following the financial crisis of 2008, it is not a new area of research. In his seminal 1776 work, *The Wealth of Nations*, Adam Smith (Smith, 1986) pointed out the productivity improvements which could be made when industrial work was broken down into discrete tasks and carried out by specialists. Writing a century later, Karl Marx described the natural inclination for industrialists to invest in automating factory processes with machinery as it was more productive than human labour and drove wages down (Marx, 1992). By the mid-twentieth century, the role of new technologies in the economic growth of nations had become an important area of research for economists, with Josef Schumpeter arguing that global economic cycles could be attributed to the development and exploitation of new technologies (Schumpeter, 1994). While there is still much debate about the extent to which technological innovations can shape macroeconomic development, there is little doubt that, for better or worse, they do impact to some degree economic growth.

A limitation of most innovation research, at least until recent years, has been its focus on product innovation. Going back to Adam Smith, the unit of study has often been changes in the physical items emerging from factories as well as the processes which went into making them. However, as the GDP of most developed economies is now dominated by receipts from the sale of services rather than factory outputs, there has been an increasing emphasis on trying to understand how innovation occurs within the service sector (Barras, 1986, 1990; Gershuny and Miles, 1983; Miles, 1993, 2005).

More recently, there has been something of a blurring between notions of what is a product and what is a service as services increasingly become bundled with products. The rise of personal computers in the 1980s and 1990s partly explains this development as software, a largely invisible artefact, became more important to users than the hardware on which it ran. As more of the software we use resides outside our computers and in the cloud, we do not even have to deal with physical media such as CDs which have traditionally been used to install software. This century, the iPod and then the smartphone epitomised the mutual reliance of hardware and software/apps with the development of ecosystems within which the technologies functioned. It was the launch of iTunes by Apple in 2001 which added real value for consumers to the iPod by creating a service which allowed users to put music onto their devices seamlessly. Similarly, app stores for Apple and Android smartphones have had the same effect with respect to software.

Case Study – Delair-Tech

Delair-Tech is a French company which manufactures unmanned aerial vehicles (UAVs), commonly referred to as drones. These are used by a variety of industries to monitor hard-to-access assets such as factory roofs, fields and large chimneys. However, it is the associated services which the company sells alongside the drones which make it particularly interesting. The company offers packages which include the aircraft, embedded sensors, a ground control station, software and training for end users to manage their own systems. Clients include the French state rail company, SNCF, which uses the drones to check lines for overhanging branches, and cognac producer Remy Martin, which monitors when its vineyards need watering. The company achieved a turnover of $3.2 million in 2015, but claimed it was growing at a rate of 200% after four years in business (Economist, 2015). Typical of many companies developing IoT-type services, Delair-Tech also offers an analytics service to help clients make sense of the data embedded in the images which its drones have collected. This can help farmers spot diseases in crops and predict yields and energy companies to detect leaks along gas and oil pipelines. Since it was founded in 2011, the company has collected billions of images and is using machine learning techniques in the analysis of this digital asset base.

Some see a similar blurring of distinctions between product and service innovations due to the development of IoT devices. A term often used to describe this phenomenon is *product-as-a-service* (PaaS) (Bucherer and Uckelmann, 2011; Linton, Klassen and Jayaraman, 2007; Mathieu, 2001; Webster Jr, 1994). While not always used in reference to the IoT, it is a phrase well suited to explain how manufacturers are increasingly having to think about the ways their customers use their products. It implies a deeper relationship between producers and consumers that does not end the moment a product is sold, but continues throughout its lifecycle. Many IoT devices naturally fall into the PaaS category as it is the data generated by the hardware which holds the value for users and which requires further services to convert it into actionable information. For example, the Nest thermostat, as we saw earlier in this book, allows owners to manage the temperature of their homes in the same way a traditional thermostat does, but it also monitors user preferences and tracks historical data. Users can access this data via an online account they set up with Nest, creating an ongoing relationship between the company and its customers. In this example, the collection, analysis and presentation of information is at the core of the value proposition for Nest purchasers. According to Blythe (2014):

> For IoT businesses the value of information, and the revenues that can be derived from that, should be based upon information flows to customers and the benefits derived by those customers, who may not be the consumers or users of the device. This introduces another important aspect, that of new customer relationships which can open up new avenues of revenue generation.
>
> (p.10)

So as the IoT embeds digital technologies in everyday items in the home and workplace, we can see a blurring of the distinction between product and service innovation. Products such as bulbs, thermostats and cars are subject to change and innovation, but are also integral to the innovations which emerge in the form of new services coming out of these products.

For companies with a tradition in the manufacture of products, this transformation can be very challenging and often requires very different business skills as their relationships with customers change.

Case Study – Autodesk

Autodesk has been making computer-aided-design (CAD) software since the early 1980s and, like a number of software companies, has moved from a standard sales model to a subscription revenue model. Its software helps manufacturers design 3D models of their products and feed those designs straight into the machines which will produce them, including 3D printers. Just as many product manufacturers are having to incorporate software into their business models to add extra layers of functionality for the emerging IoT sector, so Autodesk is adding IoT integration into its offerings. In 2015, the company bought SeeControl, which provides an IoT platform for industrial customers. SeeControl's software allows IoT developers to remotely manage their devices and offers analytics capabilities for the data which is captured. For Autodesk, this allows the company to extend the reach of its relationship with clients from just the design and manufacturing stages up to the actual usage stages where products are throwing off data. Autodesk's Fusion Connect platform is a good example of a company with an established and successful software product taking advantage of the potential of the IoT to span a broader part of the value chain in which it operates.

Lessons from the internet

The history of the internet since the World Wide Web (WWW) made it a platform for use by consumers in the mid-1990s offers a number of lessons for IoT developers in terms of where value can be delivered and profits made. The late 1990s saw large investments being made in internet businesses with the expectation that massive profits would follow those companies which were able to move traditional retail businesses onto the web. The collapse in confidence in many of these companies in the dot com bust of the early 2000s led many, perhaps reasonably, to conclude that the internet had been over-hyped and that it did not really offer significant commercial potential. Services such as email and web browsing had a utility value to domestic and business users, but there were no clear opportunities to profit from them. The exception was the provision of internet connectivity itself, but this was becoming commoditised and required significant capital investments by the telecommunication companies which offered it.

However, as the web became embedded in people's lives as a platform for finding information and communicating with friends, so opportunities for building business models around this new form of behaviour started to emerge. One of the early successes was Google, which was able to monetise the users of its search engine. Google launched its search engine in the late 1990s and it quickly became apparent it offered superior search results to its competitors through the use of its patented PageRank algorithm. Using links between different web pages as a proxy for the quality of web content, Google was able to dramatically increase the relevance and precision of search results for users. Within a few years, Google had become the world's favourite search engine, delivering billions of searches every day. Financial success followed in the early 2000s when the company started placing contextually relevant advertisements next to search results and charging advertisers when users clicked on their ads. Companies place bids with Google for how much they are prepared to pay for specific search keywords and this helps determine which ads will appear on search results pages. For advertisers, this offers a very targeted way of reaching consumers and only having to pay when someone clicks on their ads as opposed to the traditional method of paying media owners for simply showing their advertising messages irrespective of whether a user interacts with them. This model has proven particularly profitable for Google with advertising revenues providing more than 90% of the company's total revenues of $75 billion for 2015 (Sterling, 2016). So what lessons might the example of Google have for companies thinking about developing an IoT business model? Perhaps the key lesson is that the service delivered to end users may not directly be the revenue source for a company. While the value Google provided consumers was the provision of more accurate web search results, there is no evidence that users will pay for such a service. The revenue model for Google is based on the value that those searches and the people behind them offer to third parties. When someone enters the words 'car insurance' or 'chicken recipes' into a search engine, they are signalling an intention which has a monetary value to companies providing those products or services. Google is selling that data to the highest bidder in real time in the micro seconds before it serves up the search result pages. By acting as the gatekeeper for billions of search queries it has created a highly profitable advertising business.

Another highly successful gatekeeper on the internet is Facebook. The company has been able to leverage network effects to create the world's largest social networking service. Network effects were described in Chapter 3 and, where exploited, allow companies to use their customer bases as a way to lock in existing users as well as attract new ones. The core value proposition to Facebook users is not just the technical capability to share information with other users but, more importantly, the knowledge that one's friends and family are very likely to be on the service. It would not be technically challenging for a competitor to build a Facebook-like service, indeed many have tried, but it would be extremely difficult to build a critical mass of users from which to exploit network effects. There is very little incentive for anyone to join a social network which is not used by at least a proportion of their contacts. From the perspective of commercial competition, Facebook in 2016 is in a highly defensible position. Of course, new entrants will attempt to change this and Facebook has recognised it is not unassailable as seen by its purchase of potential competitors Instagram in 2012 and WhatsApp in 2014.

Platforms as business models for the IoT

The notion of technological platforms upon which successful businesses can be built was discussed in Chapter 3. The PC was shown to have been a highly profitable platform for Microsoft and Intel, and the internet itself through its technical design can be seen as a broader platform upon which numerous businesses have been built (Zittrain, 2008). Google and Facebook could be described as advertising platforms as they provide highly targetable groups of consumers to marketers. As Microsoft and Intel demonstrated, control of a technology platform can provide companies with more defensible positions particularly at a time when many ICTs are becoming commoditised and, as a consequence, much cheaper. The technology consulting firm Accenture (2015) believes that:

> [D]igital industry platforms are driving the next major wave of technology and business change. . .. The elimination of barriers – in terms of the technology, cost, and time associated with traditional IT infrastructure and application development – is the primary force driving and enabling this change.
>
> (p.55)

In their study of technology platforms across a range of industries, Baldwin and Woodard (2008) note that they can exist within firms as product lines, between firms as multi-component systems and as multi-sided markets. While these platforms may look very different to outside observers as well as to those operating within them, the authors argue that a common link unifies them. Despite being complex systems, the platforms themselves tend to remain relatively stable, but it is their components which interface with outside elements that offer the greatest stability in terms of their technical evolution. This stability is essential to instil confidence amongst third parties wishing to develop complementary products and services which can work with the platform. Therefore, they argue, whoever controls these interfaces, in effect, controls the platform. The importance of stable interfaces to platforms is exemplified by the success of the internet as a communications and information-sharing platform. The backbone infrastructure of the internet has evolved significantly over the past 30 years from being a largely academic network linking universities and research centres to one which now is at the heart of most telecommunication networks and reaches into billions of homes and businesses. Despite these dramatic changes, the TCP/IP protocols which determine how devices connect to the internet have remained extremely stable, which has encouraged the raft of innovations that sit on top of the internet and which we now take for granted. This stability combined with the network effects often associated with the success of technology platforms can create the environment needed for rapid innovation to occur as users and developers congregate around successful technologies.

However, there is a potential conflict for companies wishing to profit from the development of technology platforms. The interfaces around a platform which allow third parties to develop complementary products and services for it need to open enough for them to do this in a relatively low-cost and friction-free way, but not to open so much that the platform owner loses control of its development. The success of the internet owes much to the fact that the TCP/IP protocols are not owned by any single commercial entity but are open standards which anyone can freely use. This is a challenge which IoT platform developers are struggling with as they develop and refine their business models in ways that will encourage developers to come on board whilst maintaining enough control to ensure stable revenue streams.

Case Study – Bosch

The German precision engineering company Bosch dates back to 1886 and is now a multibillion-euro company manufacturing products for the automotive, industrial and consumer sectors from power generators and windscreen wipers to electric drills and belt sanders. Like many large industrial firms, the company is making strategic investments to ensure it can integrate IoT functionality into its products. In 2016, the company announced the launch of the Bosch Cloud to offer its IoT suite of services to customers on a remote basis. Bosch's IoT strategy is part of the broader German Industrie 4.0 initiative which combines public-sector and corporate efforts to ensure Germany is a leading player in what many are calling the Fourth Industrial Revolution. Applications for Bosch's IoT Suite include solutions for asparagus farmers to track the temperature of their plants under the ground via a smartphone app, the real-time location tracking of tools used by engineers for aircraft maintenance and robotic lawnmowers controllable by users' phones. The company's ambition is that every product it manufactures will be connectable to its IoT Cloud by 2020 (Seppala, 2016).

Compared to the relatively simple architecture of the PC and even the Android and iOS smartphone platforms, the IoT is a far more complex environment for developers to create stable and profitable platforms. This is partly due to the fragmented nature of the IoT in terms of the industries and processes it spans, but is also a result of the commoditisation of many of the layers in the IoT technology stack. Open-source software has played a part in this commoditisation, as has the falling cost of computing components, which is inevitable in any industry which has reached mass adoption and experienced fierce competition amongst suppliers. IoT industry analyst Allmendinger (2016) is critical of many of the companies, established and new entrants, which claim to be developing defensible platforms for this emerging sector. He cites a number of key pre-conditions which platform developers need to incorporate if they are to stand any chance of success. These include platforms which are device and communications agnostic thus providing a stable basis for development opportunities by third parties and, consequently, more rapid adoption by end users. Allmendinger also believes that the services platforms offer in the industrial space need to be "end-to-end" which offer managed solutions thus reducing the complexity for clients. Thirdly, platforms need to be easily scalable as client needs grow and readily accessible tools need to be made available to encourage communities of developers to build applications and solutions around the offering.

A number of companies appear to be building out IoT platforms across different parts of the technology stack and attempting to build business models which both encourage third party developers to come on board whilst also maintaining enough control to create customer value and ensure stable revenue streams. Bosch is building an IoT cloud service which aims to provide the end-to-end managed solutions advocated by Allmendinger while C3 IoT is providing a platform focused on helping energy companies manage and draw insights from their data streams. GE's Predix IoT platform is partnering with a number of large companies, including Amazon, Softbank and Cisco, to offer complete solutions for clients in the broader industrial space and who wish to develop hosted applications for business intelligence.

Case Study – Progressive Insurance

The US-based Progressive Group of Insurance Companies was founded in 1937 and offers a range of car and household insurance services. In the United States, it is a market leader in the use of telematics to track the behaviour of drivers. Its Snapshot service allows users to plug a small dongle into the OBD-II port on their cars which tracks how far the car has been driven and at what times and the braking patterns of the driver. This data is transmitted to Progressive, which then rewards safe drivers with up to a 30% discount on their premiums. By 2014, the company claimed its Snapshot users were paying more than $2 billion in premiums and had tracked more than 10 billion miles of driving over the previous 10 years (Hocking et al., 2014). While Snapshot, and the similar services offered by other insurance companies, may be attractive to safe drivers, there are issues for the established business model of the insurance industry, which is based on the pooling of risk. By offering discounts for safe driving, such companies risk reducing the profitability of such customers which have traditionally subsidised less safe drivers. However, from a road user perspective, the prospect of other people driving their cars more safely because of the financial incentive for doing so may be appealing.

IoT value creation

While the building of platforms may be a strategy for many IoT developers in their pursuit of a sustainable business model, this does not guarantee that any value created from such an approach can be profitably monetised. As we have seen throughout the previous sections, information is at the heart of the IoT and finding ways to persuade consumers, both domestic and industrial, to pay for information has become difficult in the internet age. In the consumer space, news publishers have struggled since the 1990s to successfully charge for their services. Many users have come to expect information to be free when accessed via the internet, although there are signs this may be changing. In the United Kingdom, a number of newspaper groups have begun putting up paywalls around their content and, at the quality end of the market at least, this has started to pay off. The news publishers and their struggles to adapt to the internet may hold lessons for companies which have the production, sale and analysis of information as a component of their business models.

An important lesson for any company hoping to profit from the commercial exploitation of information is to appreciate how information differs from other strategic resources used by companies. Moody and Walsh (1999) have defined what they call the seven "laws of information" which can help IoT developers better understand how value creation can be derived from the data their systems are producing. The seven laws of information comprise:

Law 1 – Unlike physical products, information can be shared with others without any loss of value.
Law 2 – The value of information increases with use and offers no value if not used at all.
Law 3 – Information is perishable and loses value over time.
Law 4 – The value of information increases with accuracy.
Law 5 – Information increases in value when combined with other information.
Law 6 – More information is not necessarily better.
Law 7 – Unlike physical products, information is not depletable.

These unique characteristics of information and the implications they have for pricing models in the information age were elaborated on in more detail by Shapiro and Varian (1998) in their playbook of rules for companies planning to offer digital information products and services. Applying these rules and the seven laws, Bucherer and Uckelmann (2011) have devised a set of requirements which will help IoT developers develop value propositions for their offerings. They argue that such companies need to:

- Provide the right information by linking unique identifiers to physical products;
- Ensure the information is appropriately granular to provide clarity and insight;
- Ensure the information is in the right condition in terms of accuracy, aggregated with other sources and formally defined from a semantic perspective so it can be processed and analysed;
- Provide timely information to meet client needs whether this is real-time or historic;
- Ensure the information is easily accessible across the networks being used;
- Price the information appropriately with a high degree of price transparency so that clients can see they are paying for the information rather than the supporting infrastructure which is delivering the data.

In his extensive research on the evolution of the IoT and the business models driving innovation in this sector, Morrish (2015) paints a picture of a fragmented landscape where data services will be behind the realisation of a more integrated IoT. He argues that the industrial IoT in 2015 and for at least the next few years is best described as "Intranets of Things". These are islands of connectivity where M2M solutions are being deployed within specific companies for very well defined purposes and the information being generated is not generally accessible to outside parties. While these "intranets of things" may be well suited to meeting precise organisational objectives, they do not accord with the requirements of Bucherer and Uckelmann (2011). In line with these requirements, Morrish believes that:

> The natural next step for integrating these solutions into the 'outside world' is to consider the integration of such 'Intranets of Things' to what could be regarded as 'adjacent' products, services and, of course, adjacent Intranets of Things.
>
> (Morrish, 2015, p.1)

Necessary for these Intranets of Things to begin connecting with each other is, Morrish argues, the common ownership of data sources or a shared interest to pool data amongst the owners. Once this occurs, he claims, the next stage towards a fully realised IoT will emerge and could be described as "Subnets of Things". However, new players will need to emerge to facilitate this in the form of Data Service Exchanges (DSEs). These, according to Morrish, are entities that intermediate and support interconnection within and between Subnets of Things. They may operate on a variety of commercial models with different pricing structures or may be set up as cooperatives for the mutual benefit of the data owners.

From a business perspective, the establishment of DSEs has an inherent logic and would go a long way to meeting Bucherer and Uckelmann's six requirements. DSEs would be able to deliver value at all levels of the technology stack from hardware manufacturers and their need for standardised frameworks to create connectable products up to the backend analytics providers and their need for stable and consistent data sources.

Challenges for IoT business model creation

So far in this chapter we have seen how business models are a useful way to understand how firms make their profits in the context of delivering value to customers. The internet has presented new opportunities and threats to companies and their business models, particularly those which have information at their centre. Technology platforms have been used successfully by a number of companies to deliver value as well as to exploit network effects and build highly defensible positions in the marketplace. In the context of the IoT, particularly the industrial IoT, data is a driver of value, but the nature of information imposes different rules on companies than those experienced by product manufacturers. For the IoT to become a reality, new mechanisms and organisations are needed to make sure that the right data is available in the right formats to the people who need it.

One of the key challenges for companies operating in the IoT space is to decide whether they are product manufacturers or data companies or something in between. To the casual observer, this may seem a strange and rather simple issue for any company to decide. Surely it is obvious what business a company is in, but in the emerging world of the IoT, the lines between products and services are blurring. Nest,[1] a company mentioned in previous sections, is a good example of how the business model it is operating to may not be what it seems. While Nest users have to purchase their smart thermostat or domestic surveillance camera for approximately $200 depending on the vendor and installation arrangements, product sales are not the only revenue stream for the company. Customers wanting to access historical video footage from their Nest Cams have to pay monthly or yearly subscriptions starting at $10 per month. This subscription model provides a recurring revenue source for Nest which also locks customers in to the service over the product's lifecycle. Less visible to Nest users is the revenue the company receives from energy providers for providing access to data generated by the thermostats. According to Blythe (2014), Nest receives approximately $40 per installation per year from these providers. In terms of the company's business model, Nest has claimed that income from energy providers for access to these data will eventually outstrip revenue from product sales and run into the hundreds of millions of dollars per year (Dillet, 2014). Energy companies are willing to pay this money so they can have access to real-time as well as historical energy usage within households and, as a consequence, be able to manage their generating plants and power grids more efficiently.

While Nest, as a new entrant to the thermostat market, may be able to build an information-based business model, other established technology companies may struggle to adapt their businesses to the new environment. This may be partly due to their lack of experience in providing services as well as or instead of physical products, or it may be because they believe their existing business models are suited to an IoT world. Many highly profitable companies fail to recognise that what may have worked in the past with respect to the industries they operate in and their product development cycles may not work in the future. This could be particularly true for companies affected by the IoT and the dynamics of a rapidly changing technology landscape. Christensen (1997) described this problem or dilemma in his seminal work on why outwardly successful companies may believe they are doing all the right things to maintain their success but are actually missing vital opportunities which newer entrants are exploiting. In many cases, he argues, by the time the company has realised this it is too late and competitors have firmly established themselves in the market. The subtitle of Christensen's book, "When new technologies cause great firms to fail", are words of caution for any company which does not think the IoT will have an impact on its operations. At the core of his hypothesis is the notion that companies which put too great a focus on meeting their customers' current needs while ignoring what customers may want in the future and adapting their offerings and business models accordingly will find themselves outmanoeuvred by newer and nimbler competitors. "Disruptive" innovations, as he calls them, in the computer hard disk drive industry in the 1980s and 1990s caught out a number of large companies in the sector which failed to exploit the move to newer and more efficient formats. More recently we can see how computer chip manufacturer Intel profited from the rise of the PC until recently, but did not foresee the rapid growth of mobile devices and their requirements for less power-intensive processors. ARM, a British company, was able to exploit this demand through its RISC architecture and its business model which centred on licensing chip designs to third parties rather than producing them itself. While Intel's chips are used in a very small number of phones and tablets, ARM has managed to take the lion's share of this sector, with almost 90% of portable devices containing ARM-designed chips equating to the manufacture of 15 billion processors in 2015 (Beddard, 2016). With its requirement for energy-efficient chips, the IoT presents a massive opportunity for ARM and it is a market which the company is actively pursuing. However, Intel, perhaps having learned its lesson with the tablet and smartphone sector, is also actively targeting the potential offered by the IoT. In 2016, it announced it was licensing chip designs from ARM, marking a radical departure from its focus on the x86 architecture which has underpinned its processor design since the late 1970s. In terms of Intel's approach to the IoT, this gives it a better chance to manufacture chips for the 'things' at the edge of the networks. However, according to IoT analyst Higginbotham (2016), while Intel hopes to get its ARM-designed chips into the 'things', it also plans to develop the market for its x86 chips in devices which the 'things' connect to and which have different power requirements. The success or not of this strategy will take a number of years to play out, but highlights the challenges facing large technology companies as they try to adapt to the IoT landscape. In Intel's case, it seems unlikely it will be able to recreate the success of its PC business model where it dominated a single platform alongside Microsoft. The IoT will require multiple platforms to address the needs of different industries and consumers as well as the technical requirements of segments of the IoT technology stack.

From hardware- to software-focused business models

For Intel, the key challenge the IoT poses is the change in requirements from purchasers of computer chips. While this may be a complex technological hurdle to overcome, for Intel, its core business is still in the manufacture of microprocessors. For a number of other industrial companies, the IoT is forcing them to radically alter their business models from ones centred on the design, manufacture and sale of hardware to products and services driven by software. The leading US venture capital firm, Andreessen Horowitz, coined the term "software is eating the world" to describe this shift. The firm's co-founder and creator of the Netscape web browser, Marc Andreessen, explained what he means by this phrase:

> My own theory is that we are in the middle of a dramatic and broad technological and economic shift in which software companies are poised to take over large swathes of the economy. More and more major businesses and industries are being run on software and delivered as online services – from movies to agriculture to national defense.
>
> (Andreessen, 2011)

Andreessen gives the example of Amazon's dominance of the US book retail sector at the expense of traditional retailer, Borders, which operated more than 500 stores and went into liquidation in 2011. While Borders clung to its business model of selling physical books from outlets, Amazon used a software-based business model to sell books online as well as ebooks via its Kindle platform.

According to Porter and Heppelmann (2015), this scenario is being played out across a number of industries as industrial firms struggle to adapt to embedding software-driven processes into their business models. He cites the examples of Daimler, Airbus and GE, which are shifting their design teams from being dominated by mechanical engineers to teams led by software engineers. Building software and communications technology into products allows new levels of service and revenue streams to be generated. Porter cites Xerox's move to making smarter photocopies which can remotely monitor usage, automatically order new toner and paper supplies and allow the company to charge on a usage basis rather than just for the sale of copiers themselves. Usage-based models have existed in the photocopier market for a number of years, but the real-time tracking of usage allows for more accurate billing and an enhanced service for customers. This model is now extending into the domestic market with computer printer manufacturer HP selling connected printers which can automatically order new ink and toner supplies from HP when they run low. Aside from the potential for new subscription-based revenue models, the data these systems generate can help with product development by providing manufacturers with valuable information about the usage patterns of customers and maintenance requirements of the hardware. This can feed into the design of improved products, creating a virtuous circle of improvement and customer satisfaction for those companies which get it right.

Note

1 Nest is an oft-used example of an IoT company and there is a danger of it being over-hyped as a flagship for this emerging sector. Key staff departures in 2016 and disappointing sales perhaps indicate there is not the public enthusiasm for smart thermostats that many people predicted. However, whatever the future of the Nest product line, the company and its takeover by Google in 2014 presents a number of interesting lessons for anyone interested in the commercial aspects of the IoT.

References

Accenture, 2015. Digital Business Era: Stretch Your Boundaries. *Accenture.* [online]. Available at: www.accenture.com/us-en/Pages/insight-technology-vision-2015.aspx.

Allmendinger, G., 2016. The Shifting Sources of Value Creation and Profitability in the Internet of Things Arena. *Harbor Research*. Available at: http://harborresearch.com/the-shifting-sources-of-value-creation-and-profitability-in-the-internet-of-things-arena/.

Andreessen, M., 2011. Why software is eating the world. *Wall Street Journal.* [online] 20 Aug. Available at: www.wsj.com/articles/SB10001424053111903480904576512250915629460.

Baldwin, C.Y. and Woodard, C.J., 2008. The Architecture of Platforms: A Unified View. *Harvard Business School Finance Working Paper (09–034)*. [online]. Available at: http://papers.ssrn.com/sol3/papers.cfm?abstract_id=1265155.

Barras, R., 1986. Towards a theory of innovation in services. *Research Policy*, 15(4), pp.161–173.

Barras, R., 1990. Interactive innovation in financial and business services: The vanguard of the service revolution. *Research Policy*, 19(3), pp.215–237.

Beddard, R., 2016. Share Sleuth: Tech Titan ARM on Sale. *Money Observer.* [online]. Available at: www.moneyobserver.com/our-analysis/share-sleuth-tech-titan-arm-sale.

Blythe, C., 2014. Business models for value generation in the Internet of Things. In: *Data-and Value-Driven Software Engineering with Deep Customer Insight*. Proceedings of the Seminar No. 58314308. Ed. Jürgen Münch. Helsinki: University of Helsinki, pp.8–15.

Bucherer, E., Eisert, U. and Gassmann, O., 2012. Towards systematic business model innovation: Lessons from product innovation management. *Creativity and Innovation Management*, 21(2), pp.183–198.

Bucherer, E. and Uckelmann, D., 2011. Business models for the Internet of Things. In *Architecting the Internet of Things*. [online]. Springer, pp.253–277. Available at: http://link.springer.com/chapter/10.1007/978–3–642–19157–2_10.

Christensen, C.M., 1997. *The Innovator's Dilemma: When New Technologies Cause Great Firms to Fail 1st*. 1st ed. Boston, MA: Harvard Business Review Press.

Dillet, R., 2014. Nest Uses Its Data to Turn Electric Utilities into Cash Cows. *TechCrunch*. [online]. Available at: http://social.techcrunch.com/2014/04/18/nest-uses-its-data-to-turn-electric-utilities-into-cash-cows/.

Economist, 2015. Airborne Innovation. *The Economist*, 5 Dec., p.69.

Fleisch, E., Weinberger, M. and Wortmann, F., 2015. Business models and the Internet of Things. In *Interoperability and Open-Source Solutions for the Internet of Things*. [online]. Springer, pp.6–10. Available at: http://link.springer.com/chapter/10.1007/978–3–319–16546–2_2.

Gershuny, J. and Miles, I., 1983. *The New Service Economy: The Transformation of Employment in Industrial Societies*. London: Praeger.

Higginbotham, S., 2016. Intel's IoT Strategy Is Becoming Clear. *Medium*. [online]. Available at: https://medium.com/@gigastacey/intels-iot-strategy-is-becoming-clear-ecbc88156a0b.

Hocking, J., Wood, A., Dally, N., Pan, K. and Lin, B., 2014. *Insurance and Technology: Evolution and Revolution in a Digital World*. Blue Papers. New York: Morgan Stanley. Kiel, D., Arnold, C., Collisi, M. and Voigt, K.-I., 2016. The impact of the industrial Internet of Things on established business models. In *Proceedings of the International Association for Management of Technology*. [online]. IAMOT 2016. Orlando, Florida: International Association for Management of Technology, pp.673–695. Available at: www.industrial-management.wiso.uni-erlangen.de/IAMOT_2016_paper_65_Kiel.pdf.

Linton, J.D., Klassen, R. and Jayaraman, V., 2007. Sustainable supply chains: An introduction. *Journal of Operations Management*, 25(6), pp.1075–1082.

Marx, K., 1992. *Das Kapital*. London: Penguin Classics.

Mathieu, V., 2001. Service strategies within the manufacturing sector: benefits, costs and partnership. *International Journal of Service Industry Management*, 12(5), pp.451–475.

Miles, I., 1993. Services in the new industrial economy. *Futures*, 25(6), pp.653–672.

Miles, I., 2005. Innovation in services. In: *The Oxford Handbook of Innovation*. Ed. J. Fagerberg, D.C. Mowery and R.R. Nelson. Oxford: Oxford University Press, pp.433–458.

Moody, D.L. and Walsh, P., 1999. Measuring the value of Information: an asset valuation approach. In *ECIS*. [online]. Seventh European Conference on Information Systems (ECIS'99). Copenhagen Business School, Frederiksberg, Denmark: Association for Information Systems, pp.496–512.

Morrish, J., 2015. The Emergence of Data Service Exchanges: Liquidity for the IoT. *Machina Research*. [online]. Available at: https://machinaresearch.com/report/the-emergence-of-data-service-exchanges-liquidity-for-the-iot/.

Osterwalder, A. and Pigneur, Y., 2010. *Business Model Generation: A Handbook for Visionaries, Game Changers, and Challengers*. 1st ed. Hoboken, NJ: John Wiley & Sons.

Porter, M.E. and Heppelmann, J.E., 2015. How Smart, Connected Products Are Transforming Companies. *Harvard Business Review*. [online]. Available at: https://hbr.org/2015/10/how-smart-connected-products-are-transforming-companies.

Schumpeter, J., 1994. *Capitalism, Socialism and Democracy*. London: Routledge.

Seppala, T., 2016. Bosch Is Building Its Own Internet of Things Cloud Network. *Engadget*. [online]. Available at: www.engadget.com/2016/03/10/bosch-iot-cloud/.

Shapiro, C. and Varian, H.R., 1998. *Information Rules: A Strategic Guide to the Network Economy*. Boston, MA: Harvard Business Review Press.

Smith, A., 1986. *The Wealth of Nations*. London: Penguin Books.

Sterling, G., 2016. Google Revenues Beat Expectations with $21.3B in Q4 And $75B in 2015. *Marketing Land.* [online]. Available at: http://marketingland.com/google-revenues-beat-expectations-with-21–3-billion-in-q4-and-75-billion-in-2015–162152.

Teece, D.J., 2010. Business models, business strategy and innovation. *Long Range Planning*, 43(2–3), pp.172–194.

Webster Jr, F.E., 1994. Executing the new marketing concept. *Marketing Management*, 3(1), p.8.

Zittrain, J., 2008. *The Future of the Internet*. London: Penguin Books.

6 IoT challenges

Introduction

The core technologies and economic factors driving the IoT have been discussed in the previous sections. It should be clear that many of the technical foundations for the IoT to flourish are in place while many companies are still struggling to create new or adapt existing business models to take advantage of this new landscape. On the industrial side, real IoT solutions are being rolled out and delivering measurable benefits to businesses. Domestic IoT applications are at an earlier stage and, in many cases, consumers are often not convinced of the need for some of the products on the market. However, many of these issues will be solved by easier-to-use products being marketed at lower prices to attract less tech-savvy consumers. As Rogers (2003) has shown through his numerous case studies, once innovative new technologies start to be used by early adopters and their benefits can be seen by the broader market, then mass adoption is more likely. New technologies bring with them much uncertainty, particularly those which impact our daily lives. The first mobile phones launched in the early 1980s cost several thousands of pounds to purchase alongside expensive monthly subscriptions and call charges. The Motorola DynaTAC 8000X cost $4,000 in 1984 (more than $9,000 in 2016 money) with a monthly subscription of $50 ($115 in 2016 money) with calls costing more than 40 cents a minute (approximately $1 in 2016 money) (Wolpin, 2014). Such devices were clearly not for everyone, and even the telecom service providers were uncertain as to who would buy them. In the early 1980s, AT&T commissioned consulting firm McKinsey to predict the likely sales of mobile phones. The company estimated that due to high costs, poor coverage and very limited battery life, the total global market would not exceed 900,000 units (Economist, 1999). As a consequence, AT&T decided not to enter the market, an expensive mistake it rectified later. By the end of 2015, there were an estimated 4.4 billion mobile phone users, 60% of the world's population (Statista, 2016). Falling component costs, better network coverage and improved battery life, as well as the innate desire for people to communicate with each other, ensured mobile devices soon became a part of our lives. Betting against a technology because the early iterations of it are not perfect is often a mistake, and this is equally true of many IoT products and services which are still at the early stages of development.

However, there are a number of broader, not solely technical problems which need to be resolved before the IoT has a chance of achieving the adoption levels we have seen with other technologies such as the PC and mobile phone. These centre on the interrelated issues of privacy, security and regulation. As computing and communication technologies become ever more embedded in our daily lives at work and in the home, the potential for adverse consequences grows. This might be the hacking of IoT systems in industrial settings to take control of energy supply systems or the leaking, accidental or otherwise, of sensitive personal data from health monitoring devices. In many ways, these problems are nothing new and we have seen similar issues arise from the growth of personal computing and the internet. However, it is the sheer scale of what the IoT promises which is raising concerns amongst consumers, developers and regulators. The solutions are not simply technological ones, but will rely on a combination of technical fixes, new regulations and a user base more aware of its role in securing the IoT.

Lessons from the past

It is often assumed that the internet brought with it new and unprecedented problems associated with the rapid rise of a global communications network. However, as Standage (1999) has shown, the Victorians had to grapple with similar problems in the nineteenth century with the invention of the electric telegraph system. This network quickly grew from its first deployments in the 1840s and was, in many ways, more significant than the internet 150 years later. For the first time, people could communicate with each other out of line of sight and in real time. Once international lines had been laid under the ocean in the 1850s and 1860s, the world was a smaller place and global communication, for those who could afford it, was transformed. While this offered many benefits for businesses, it also led to the rise of new problems, particularly around fraud. Commenting on this in 1888, Inspector John Bonfield of the Chicago police stated to the *Chicago Herald*:

> It is a well-known fact that no other section of the population avail themselves more readily and speedily of the latest triumphs of science than the criminal class. The educated criminal skims the cream from every new invention if he can make use of it.
>
> (Standage, 1999, p.100)

Even before the electric telegraph, two French bankers were caught in the 1830s bribing operators of the signal-based optical telegraph to obtain advance information on movements on the French stock exchange which they could use to their financial advantage (Gatherer and Auslander, 2002). One of the first frauds perpetrated over the electric telegraph centred on horse racing. Before the telegraph, results from horse races could take hours and sometimes days to reach bookmakers in other parts of the country. In the 1840s, according to Standage (1999), a man went into the telegraph office next to where the Derby horse race had just taken place and sent a seemingly innocuous message to a friend: 'Your luggage and tartan will be safe by the next train.' However, the word 'tartan' was a secret code for the friend to place a bet on the race with a bookmaker who did not yet know the result, resulting in a substantial profit for the gambler. Secret codes and encrypted telegraph messages became more popular as users wanted to keep the contents of their communications confidential. In some countries, the use of such codes became illegal, and in Prussia, a law was passed forcing telegraph operators to keep copies of all the messages they sent. These activities are all very reminiscent of issues surrounding fraud and encryption on the internet today.

So what lessons do the telegraph, the telephone and the early days of the internet hold for the emerging IoT? Perhaps the first lesson is related to the quote from the Chicago policeman. Wherever a technology can used to exploit a weakness in a system for financial gain, it is inevitable that someone will do it. In the United Kingdom, online banking fraud rose by 48% in 2014 compared to 2013 as more people did their banking over the internet (Peachey, 2015), while 3.8 million people in 2014 in England and Wales were the victims of online fraud (Croft, 2015). In 2011, Sony suffered an attack on its network via the internet with the personal data, including, in some cases, the credit card details, of 77 million of its PlayStation Network being stolen (Baker and Finkle, 2011). Often the extent of such illegal hacks is never known or underestimated by the companies which have been attacked. In 2012, it was thought that 6.5 million passwords had been stolen from the social network LinkedIn. However, it was only in 2016 that the company revealed more than 117 million passwords had been taken and that these data were being sold on the internet (Pagliery, 2016). An obvious lesson for any company which holds large amounts of personal data is to make sure that the latest technologies are being deployed to make them as safe as possible. It is not unreasonable for end users to assume this to be the case, particularly with larger companies that have the resources to do this. However, the example of TalkTalk, the UK internet service provider (ISP), is a cautionary tale for anyone who assumes their data are safe. In 2015, the addresses of more than 150,000 of the company's customers were stolen, with 15,000 of these including the bank account numbers and sort codes

(Farrell, 2015). Rather than a well-planned attack by cybercrime experts, it later emerged that the attack had been perpetrated by teenage boys who had exploited the TalkTalk website to expose unencrypted customer data. The following section will explore in more detail the key specific privacy, security and regulatory issues surrounding the IoT and their implications for business.

Privacy and the IoT

The internet has changed many people's perceptions of personal privacy over the past 20 years. Before the internet became a network for the masses, most people's concerns over privacy centred on whether to allow the telephone company to publish their name, phone number and address in the telephone directory or wondering why the *Reader's Digest* kept sending them special offers.[1] In a world where more than 1.5 billion people are regularly posting updates about their location and posting photographs of themselves on public social networks, as well as posting intimate questions on search engines, something has clearly changed. Dutton and colleagues (2013) see the dispersed nature of the IoT as posing particular issues in terms of personal privacy and argue that more emphasis needs to be given to research into social aspects of this new technology:

> Social and legal issues are likely to be shaped by the ways in which services are provided, such as via cloud computing or more decentralised storage and retrieval at the end of the pipe. Research needs to focus on embedding this full range of arrangements for provision to examine such issues as whether privacy and data protection are exacerbated in some IoT infrastructures, such as in the cloud. Where is the data collected, analysed and archived, by whom and under whose control? With whom is it shared and under what provisions?
>
> (Dutton et al., 2013, p.6)

This points to a central problem with the IoT and personal privacy, particularly in the domestic sphere: how aware are people of the devices and systems around them in terms of the data they are collecting and sharing with others? When we post something to Facebook or Instagram, we do so with the expectation that others will see it. When we tell our smart television to find a particular film on Netflix or track our running progress with our smart watch, do we know where those data are going and who has access to them? According to Farr (2016), the Fitbit fitness bracelet can tell, based on their vital signs, if users are pregnant, if they are ill or if they are recovering from a hangover. As these are personal fitness gadgets, this may seem uncontroversial, but, as Farr points out, there is a growing trend, particularly in the United States, for companies to offer incentives for their employees to wear these devices. Employers are keen on this because there is evidence that people who track their fitness are more likely to stay healthy than those who don't and employees take part in these programs because their health insurance premiums can be reduced based on their physical activity as measured by the Fitbit. Suddenly the ability for Fitbits to track pregnancy, illness or hangovers may not be so attractive for the user if his/her employer can also see that data. There seems to be a grey area as to what data employers can actually see, and, claims Farr (2016), Fitbit has a privacy policy in place to protect its users' data. However, according to Lee Tien of the Electronic Frontier Foundation (EFF):[2]

> People might assume or expect that there are privacy protections but they don't know what data is being collected.
>
> (Farr, 2016, p.30)

Tien's concerns about public awareness of online data collection and the extent of the volume of information which is being collected on us by private companies is certainly not baseless. In 2011, an Austrian law student, Max Schrems, used European data protection legislation to ask Facebook what data the company held on him. He was surprised when he received a CD containing 1,200 pages of data of his online activity, including who he had 'friended' and 'unfriended' and all his personal messages, even ones he had deleted (Walker, 2015). Schrems' CD of data illustrates well the business of social media companies as well as many IoT players, and that is the business of compiling personal data and monetising it through targeted advertising, selling additional services based on user behaviour or selling the data to third parties. In a report for the World Economic Forum (WEF),[3] Schwab and colleagues (2011) argue that personal data is becoming a new "asset class" which can create value for individuals and companies, as well as broader society. However, he acknowledge that much work needs to be done to increase the transparency with which organisations use personal data so that individuals trust how their information is managed and shared. This, he claims, will be even more important if predictions about the IoT and its diffusion throughout society become a reality.

Although the EFF and the WEF agree that the IoT presents big challenges to the protection of personal privacy, the different interests they represent mean their solutions are not always the same. The EFF approaches the issue from what it sees as the interests of individual users of digital technologies and, particularly through its campaigning on copyright laws, has shown that these interests are often in conflict with the corporate supporters of the WEF.

These conflicting interests are magnified with the IoT where the potential profits from exploiting the new data assets will be, according to some critics, at the expense of the individuals creating this data. Another US-based pressure group which has raised concerns about the privacy aspects of the IoT is the Electronic Privacy Information Center (EPIC). In 2015, the organisation filed a complaint with the US Federal Trade Commission relating to Samsung's 'Smart TV' and its ability to listen in on conversations taking place near the television and other 'always on' devices used in the home (EPIC, 2016). EPIC's complaint with respect to Samsung focuses on its Smart TV's, which have a microphone to allow voice control of the television's functions by users. To many this is a useful function and not, in itself, a cause for concern. However, when EPIC researchers looked more closely at Samsung's privacy policy for this service, they noticed the following:

> Samsung may collect and your device may capture voice commands and associated texts so that we can provide you with Voice Recognition features and evaluate and improve the features. Please be aware that if your spoken words include personal or other sensitive information, that information will be among the data captured and transmitted to a third party through your use of Voice Recognition.
>
> (EPIC, 2016)

The third party to which Samsung televisions transmit these recordings is a voice recognition company called Nuance. EPIC claims a number of US laws regarding the protection of children's privacy and communications legislation are contravened by this practice. While Samsung has amended its privacy policy to clarify what data it does collect and for what purpose, EPIC's complaint raises a number of concerns. One problem is the issue of how many people actually read the terms and conditions (T&Cs) of online services they use. A US survey in 2015 revealed that less than 20% of respondents consistently read the T&Cs before signing up to a service online with more than 30% never reading them (Morrison, 2015). One of the key reasons cited in the survey for not reading T&Cs was that if you do not agree then you cannot access the service.

The 'always on' and listening issue with the IoT extends to an ever-broader range of devices and, as machine learning and voice recognition improve, will become even further embedded in our homes. Google's 'Ok Google' search command for smartphones and PC's, Apple's Siri and Amazon's Alexa are all examples of how the largest technology companies are attempting to make their digital assistants a natural part of our daily lives. While adults, in theory at least, are able to make rational decisions whether to engage with these services, children are obviously more vulnerable. In

2015, Mattel, the maker of the Barbie doll, launched 'Hello Barbie', a doll fitted with a microphone and Wi-Fi connectivity that records children's voices as they talk to it. Similar to the Samsung televisions, this data is then uploaded to a voice recognition service which allows the doll to engage in 'conversation' with the child. According to Mattel's FAQ for the toy:

> Hello Barbie has conversations with girls, and these conversations are recorded. These audio recordings are used to understand what is being said to Hello Barbie so she can respond appropriately and also to improve speech recognition for children and to make the service better. These conversations are stored securely on ToyTalk's server infrastructure and parents have the power to listen to, share, and/or delete stored recordings any time.
>
> (Mattel, 2016)

Mattel points out that the doll only records voices when it is turned on, and so is not a true 'always on' device. While this toy raises concerns for privacy amongst children, it is perhaps the potential for third parties to hack into the toy which has generated most controversy. Within months of the doll being launched, a way was found to hack into the toy so it could be used as a surveillance device which could listen in to children without their parents' consent. A security researcher in the United States found it was possible when the toy was connected to Wi-Fi to access account information, stored recordings and direct access to the microphone (Gibbs, 2015). A similar issue has been reported with wireless video cameras used to monitor babies in their cots, with users reporting hearing voices talking to their babies when they enter the nursery (Ross, 2016).

Security

These examples and the concerns raised by privacy advocates highlight a growing concern around the IoT and one which any business involved in this sector needs to be aware of. The history of technology, particularly related to computing and the internet, shows us that devices and software will only become more powerful and rich in features. As companies use artificial intelligence, machine learning and ever-more sophisticated algorithms to give their products and services a competitive advantage, the amount of personal and sensitive data flowing across the internet will increase. Embedding robust security at all levels of the IoT technology stack will be crucial to prevent fraud and engender the trust that will be vital for mass adoption to take place.

A key cause for concern with IoT security is the number of companies entering the market which do not have experience of security in a network context. Mattel is a company that has built up expertise in designing and marketing toys, not building products which can withstand attacks from determined hackers. Companies such as Yale have decades of experience in providing locks for securing buildings, but have only very recently had to grapple with the intricacies of electronic attacks on their products. It is essential that security is built into products and services at the design stage rather than as an afterthought. Speaking at a security and privacy event in New York in 2016, a legal advisor to the EFF, Nate Cardozo, sounded an exasperated note on this matter:

> Why are we putting networking in everything? Those companies that have engineering staff but no security staff don't know what to do with a vulnerability report . . . the big guys, the software companies, those are nearly always seamless. Apple knows what to do with a vulnerability report. But medical device companies? They don't have a f*****g clue.
>
> (Lomas, 2016)

According to a recent Federal Trade Commission report (FTC, 2015), when companies are designing for the IoT they should:

1 Conduct a privacy and security risk assessment;
2 Minimise the data they collect and retain from their IoT initiatives;
3 Rigorously test their products before launching to the market.

Allmendinger, Newkirk and Groopman (2016) expand on this rather generic advice and have outlined a series of steps which any company building products for the IoT should follow to maximise the robustness of their security strategy. These are:

1 Think about the security approach from the customer perspective in terms of what the solution will do, who it will report to and how it will be secured.
2 Apply a multi-layered security approach that incorporates identity, access management, access management, encryption, analytics and network security.
3 Define the lifecycle controls which will determine the management of the system, how incidents will be solved and when the system will be retired and/or updated.

Clearly security is more of an issue in some scenarios than others. Hacking into someone's smart thermostat and turning off the heating may be an inconvenience, but taking control of a self-driving car and crashing it on purpose is something very different. In March 2016, the US Department of Justice announced it was bringing charges against an Iranian hacker who had mounted a cyber-attack on the Bowman Dam in Rye, New York (Metzger and O'Donnell, 2016). According to the prosecution, the defendant gained access to the dam-monitoring data and, had the system not been switched to manual, would have been able to remotely operate the sluice gate and release millions of tons of water. In December 2015, the first reported take-down of a national power grid took place in Ukraine. Zetter (2016) describes the panic of the grid centre manager as he looked at his computer and saw the

> cursor on his computer suddenly skittered across the screen of its own accord. He watched as it navigated purposefully toward buttons controlling the circuit breakers at a substation in the region and then clicked on a box to open the breakers and take the substation offline. A dialogue window popped up on screen asking to confirm the action, and the operator stared dumbfounded as the cursor glided to the box and clicked to affirm. The operator grabbed his mouse and tried desperately to seize control of the cursor, but it was unresponsive. Then as the cursor moved in the direction of another breaker, the machine suddenly logged him out of the control panel. Although he tried frantically to log back in, the attackers had changed his password preventing him from gaining re-entry. All he could do was stare helplessly at his screen while the ghosts in the machine clicked open one breaker after another, eventually taking about 30 substations offline.
>
> (Zetter, 2016)

This chilling account highlights the risks of a connected world where network and software vulnerabilities can be exploited so directly. Less dramatic but still concerning breaches have been reported with home security systems (Moore, 2016), smart thermostats (Storm, 2014) and driverless cars (Versprille, 2015). The lesson is that if it can be hacked, it will be hacked.

Regulation and the IoT

If the IoT is to become a reality to the extent that many analyst are predicting, then a core pre-requisite is the establishment of trust amongst adopters. The previous sections have shown what is at risk in terms of the amounts of personal data which many consumer-facing IoT services generate and the seeming inability of some vendors to incorporate adequate security in their products. As with other new information and communication technologies, there is an important role for regulators to set legal frameworks for the sector to operate by. In some cases, new regulations will be required to take into account the new challenges the IoT poses, while in others existing legislation may be sufficient or require updating. It should be noted that regulators in many countries are also involved in the licensing of radio spectrum, which has an obvious impact on the development cycles of many IoT developers. This section, however, focuses on the role of regulation in the management of the data generated by the IoT in Europe and the United States. The geographic focus obviously misses developments in other parts of the world, but it offers some useful insights into how regulators and policy makers are working with industry to develop frameworks for the governance of the IoT. The leading role the United States plays in IoT innovations and the concern within the European Union for protecting personal privacy highlights the tensions as well as the common interests which exist between business and IoT developers.

European regulatory approaches

Following the Second World War, there was a concern in Europe for the protection of personal data to prevent a repeat of abuses seen under the Nazis and their use of identity records to facilitate the Holocaust. Following the United Nations' Universal Declaration of Human Rights in 1948, the European Convention on Human Rights was drafted by the Council of Europe and was enacted in 1953 (McCarty-Snead and Hilby, 2013). The European Court of Human Rights was established at the same time to provide a place where individuals can bring cases if they feel their rights under the Convention have been violated. Judgements from this court are binding in EU member states. In the context of personal privacy, it is Section 1 of Article 8 of the Convention which is most relevant and had the greatest impact on European privacy legislation:

> Everyone has the right to respect for his or her private and family life, home and correspondence.
>
> (Liberty, 2016)

Following growing concerns about the rise of computer databases in the 1960s and 1970s, pressure grew to enact specific European legislation to specify how organisations should use the personal data they were collecting. European legislation followed in the 1980s and 1990s with the passing of directives on data protection, which were enacted into national legislation in member states. In the United Kingdom, this took the form of the 1984 Data Protection Act followed by an updated version, the 1998 Data Protection Act, which was a result of a 1995 EU Directive. The UK body charged with enforcing the 1998 Act is the Information Commissioner's Office (ICO), and it has condensed the core tenets of the Act into eight principles which any organisation holding personal information must adhere to:

1 Personal data shall be processed fairly and lawfully.
2 Personal data shall be obtained only for one or more specified and lawful purposes, and shall not be further processed in any manner incompatible with that purpose or those purposes.
3 Personal data shall be adequate, relevant and not excessive in relation to the purpose or purposes for which they are processed.
4 Personal data shall be accurate and, where necessary, kept up to date.
5 Personal data processed for any purpose or purposes shall not be kept for longer than is necessary for that purpose or those purposes.
6 Personal data shall be processed in accordance with the rights of data subjects under this Act.
7 Appropriate technical and organisational measures shall be taken against unauthorised or unlawful processing of personal data and against accidental loss or destruction of, or damage to, personal data.
8 Personal data shall not be transferred to a country or territory outside the European Economic Area unless that country or territory ensures an adequate level of protection for the rights and freedoms of data subjects in relation to the processing of personal data.(ICO, 2016)

The Act also gives individuals rights to inspect records which organisations hold on them, have errors corrected and, in the case of data held for marketing purposes, have data deleted. The key message for organisations is they should only hold the data they need for specific purposes, maintain them securely and only for as long as they are needed. There are exceptions for the security services and situations where data need to be held for contractual and legal purposes such as entering into financial credit arrangements with a bank. In April 2016, the European Commission adopted the General Data Protection Regulation (GDPR), which will replace the 1995 Directive when it comes into force in May 2018 (Blackmer, 2016). While the GDPR is not radically different to the 1995 Directive it will replace, it does include some amendments which are an acknowledgement of how far technology has evolved since the 1990s. These relate to data portability and the 'right to be forgotten'. The regulation states that where data is held in a "structured and commonly used format", individuals have a right to demand it is transferred to another service provider. However, as Blackmer (2016) points out, this is rather meaningless until the European Commission adopts implementing measures to specify exactly what this means. The new 'right to be forgotten' stems from an earlier ruling by the Court of Justice of the

European Union in 2014 on a case brought by a Spanish citizen against Google. He was unhappy that information about a house repossession he had gone through in the 1990s was still showing up in search results for his name. He felt that as the matter had been resolved more than a decade before it was prejudicial to his reputation for this information to still be associated with him. The 2014 ruling, which was based on an interpretation of the 1995 Directive, was significant for three key reasons:

1 Even if the computer servers on which the data processing is taking place are outside the EU, the Directive still applies if the company operates a subsidiary in the member state which is generating revenue from advertising.
2 Search engines are 'controllers' of personal data in the sense of the Directive's definition of a data controller and, therefore, Google is subject to the Directive.
3 Individuals have the right, under certain conditions, to be forgotten where the information is inaccurate, inadequate, irrelevant or excessive for the purposes of data processing.(European Commission, 2014)

While concerns have been expressed that this right to be forgotten may allow some individuals, corrupt politicians, for example, to escape public scrutiny, it is an important precedent for European information law. The billions of data points which internet companies such as Facebook, Google and Amazon hold on individuals are amassing into vast treasure troves of personal data which, unless legally checked, will never go away. As the IoT takes hold, these data will only increase, and the ruling is an important step in giving some control back to the individuals whose personal information is the foundation of these companies' wealth.

As well as the enhanced rights granted to data subjects described earlier, the GDPR also includes three other areas with direct relevance to the IoT. According to Finlay and Madigan (2016), these are:

1 Consent – in response to concerns that obtaining consent from data subjects with some IoT devices might be difficult,[4] the regulation tightens up the responsibilities placed on data controllers in this context. Under the GDPR data controllers will have to

> demonstrate consent has been given by way of a clear affirmative act establishing a freely given, specific, informed and unambiguous indication of the data subject's agreement to the processing of his or her personal data . . . Consent cannot be presumed through the inaction of the data subject and that consent should not be regarded

> as freely given if the data subject has no genuine or free choice or is unable to refuse or withdraw consent without detriment.
>
> (Finlay and Madigan, 2016)

2. Security breaches – based on the security issues described in the previous section, the GDPR introduces a compulsory notification scheme for controllers if a security breach occurs. This will involve notifying the national supervisory authority of the breach within 72 hours and, in some instances, also contacting the affected data subjects.
3. Privacy by design and by default – although these are mentioned in the 1995 Directive, the GDPR makes them more explicit and defined. Controllers will need to demonstrate compliance at both the technical and organisational levels.

US regulatory approaches

There are clear differences in the US and European approaches to regulating around personal data. While Europe has, as discussed previously, explicit data protection regulation which cuts across industries and technologies, the United States has a more piecemeal approach with a number of federal and state-specific laws each tackling different aspects of personal data (Lee, 2014). This is partly a reflection of the importance of state legislatures in the United States, but also, perhaps, reflects a more relaxed attitude amongst many US citizens as to how organisations use their personal data. However, in the case of the IoT, concerns are beginning to come to the fore as to the volumes of data which are likely to be collected and how they will be used. This has not resulted in any new legislation, but a Federal Trade Commission report, The Internet of Things: Privacy and Security in a Connected World, (FTC, 2015), from 2015 outlined some key recommendations which were listed in an earlier section. Although these recommendations are not legally binding, according to Rouhani-Arani (2015), the FTC report

> has been released on the back of the FTC taking an active approach towards prosecuting IoT device makers for privacy and security breaches, and is likely to fuel further class actions for breach of privacy against device makers in the USA.
>
> (Rouhani-Arani, 2015)

The lack of consistency between the United States and Europe in their data protection legislation has been an issue for EU member states through the restrictions placed on companies operating in these countries and the extent to which they can move personal data outside the EU. The data protection directive and the GDPR allow for the movement of these data to companies in the United States providing they are subject to the same data protection treatment as they would be in Europe. This is commonly referred to as the Safe Harbour Agreement and has been in operation since 2000. Without this, it would not have been possible for internet companies such as Facebook and Google to hold so much personal data on European citizens on their US servers. However, in 2015, following a Court of Justice of the EU ruling, *Maximillian Schrems v Information Commissioner*,[5] ruled that the Safe Harbour arrangement was invalid as it did not protect European citizens from unwarranted US government surveillance (Robinson and Ahmed, 2015). Although a replacement agreement came into force in August 2016, the EU-US Privacy Shield, it is far from certain this will not also be subject to legal challenges by those who feel it does not go far enough in protecting personal data (Twentyman, 2016).

Notes

1 I realise this is a rather simplified, UK-centric version of events, but it is not unrealistic to assume that the situation was broadly similar in other developed economies.

2 The EFF was founded in the United States in 1990 to, in its own words, champion "user privacy, free expression, and innovation through impact litigation, policy analysis, grassroots activism, and technology development. We work to ensure that rights and freedoms are enhanced and protected as our use of technology grows" (EFF, 2016).

3 The WEF is a Sweden-based, non-profit organisation set up in 1971 to, in its own words, "demonstrate entrepreneurship in the global public interest while upholding the highest standards of governance. Moral and intellectual integrity is at the heart of everything it does" (WEF, 2016). It is the organisation which organises the annual Davos meeting for leading businesspeople and policy makers to discuss global issues.

4 It is relatively easy to obtain consent from users when the service is delivered via the web or an app; the developer can include a tick box which the user must tick before the service is delivered. When an IoT device is only a piece of hardware, this can be more difficult.

5 This is the same Max Schrems mentioned earlier in this chapter who, in 2011, uncovered the extent of personal data held on users by Facebook.

References

Allmendinger, G., Newkirk, H. and Groopman, J., 2016. *Security for the Internet of Things*. Boulder, CO: Harbor Research.

Baker, L. and Finkle, J., 2011. Sony PlayStation Suffers Massive Data Breach. *Reuters UK.* [online]. Available at: http://uk.reuters.com/article/us-sony-stoldendata-idUSTRE73P6WB20110426.

Blackmer, S., 2016. *GDPR: Getting Ready for the New EU General Data Protection Regulation.* [online]. InfoLawGroup LLP. Available at: www.infolawgroup.com/2016/05/articles/gdpr/gdpr-getting-ready-for-the-new-eu-general-data-protection-regulation/.

Croft, J., 2015. Cyber Crime and Online Fraud on the Rise. *Financial Times*. [online]. Available at: www.ft.com/cms/s/0/963d83a4–7322–11e5-a129–3fcc4f641d98.html.

Dutton, W.H., Capra, L., Ciaraldi, M., Evans, D.F., Furness, A., Graham, I., Jirotka, M., Kupai, A., Maguire, M., Matthews, N., Mowbray, M., Payne, M.K., Prendiville, A., Steinmueller, W.E. and Tyrrell, R., 2013. A roadmap for interdisciplinary research on the Internet of Things: social sciences. *SSRN Electronic Journal*. [online]. Available at: www.ssrn.com/abstract=2234664.

Economist, 1999. Cutting the Cord. *The Economist*. [online] 7 Oct. Available at: www.economist.com/node/246152.

EFF, 2016. About EFF. *Electronic Frontier Foundation*. [online]. Available at: www.eff.org/about.

EPIC, 2016. *EPIC – Samsung 'Smart TV' Complaint*. [online]. Available at: https://epic.org/privacy/internet/ftc/samsung/.

European Commission, 2014. Factsheet on the 'Right to be Forgotten' Ruling. *European Commission*. [online]. Available at: http://ec.europa.eu/justice/data-protection/files/factsheets/factsheet_data_protection_en.pdf.

Farr, C., 2016. Fitbit at Work. *Fast Company*, May, pp.27–30.

Farrell, S., 2015. Nearly 157,000 Had Data Breached in TalkTalk Cyber-Attack. *The Guardian*. [online] 6 Nov. Available at: www.theguardian.com/business/2015/nov/06/nearly-157000-had-data-breached-in-talktalk-cyber-attack [Accessed 24 Aug. 2016].

Finlay, A. and Madigan, R., 2016. GDPR and the Internet of Things: 5 Things You Need to Know. *Lexology*. [online]. Available at: www.lexology.com/library/detail.aspx?g=ba0b0d12-bae3–4e93-b832–85c15620b877.

FTC, 2015. *Internet of Things: Privacy & Security in a Connected World*. Washington, DC: Federal Trade Commission.

Gatherer, A. and Auslander, E., 2002. *The Application of Programmable DSPs in Mobile Communications*. New York: John Wiley & Sons.

Gibbs, S., 2015. Hackers Can hijack Wi-Fi Hello Barbie to Spy on Your Children. *The Guardian*. [online] 26 Nov. Available at: www.theguardian.com/technology/2015/nov/26/hackers-can-hijack-wi-fi-hello-barbie-to-spy-on-your-children.

ICO, 2016. *Data Protection Principles*. [online]. Available at: https://ico.org.uk/for-organisations/guide-to-data-protection/data-protection-principles/.

Lee, P., 2014. How Do EU and US Privacy Regimes Compare? *Field Fisher Privacy Law Blog*. [online]. Available at: http://privacylawblog.fieldfisher.com/2014/how-do-eu-and-us-privacy-regimes-compare/.

Liberty, 2016. Article 8 Right to a Private and Family Life. *Liberty Human Rights*. [online]. Available at: www.liberty-human-rights.org.uk/human-rights/what-are-human-rights/human-rights-act/article-8-right-private-and-family-life.

Lomas, N., 2016. The Internet of Things Is a Security Nightmare, Warns EFF. *TechCrunch*. [online]. Available at: http://social.techcrunch.com/2016/05/09/the-internet-of-things-is-security-nightmare-warns-eff/.

Mattel, 2016. FAQ. *Hello Barbie*. [online]. Available at: http://hellobarbiefaq.mattel.com/faq/.

McCarty-Snead, S. and Hilby, A., 2013. *Research Guide to European Data Protection Law*. Legal Research Series. Berkeley, CA: University of California, Berkeley.

Metzger, R. and O'Donnell, R.J., 2016. Internet of Things: When Cyberattacks Have Physical Effects. *Federal Times*. [online]. Available at: www.federaltimes.com/story/government/solutions-ideas/2016/04/08/internet-things-when-cyberattacks-have-physical-effects/82787430/.

Moore, N., 2016. Hacking into Homes: 'Smart Home' Security Flaws Found in Popular System. *University of Michigan News*. [online]. Available at: www.ns.umich.edu/new/multimedia/videos/23748-hacking-into-homes-smart-home-security-flaws-found-in-popular-system?utm_source=feedburner&utm_medium=feed&utm_campaign=Feed+umns-videospodcastsslideshows+University+of+Michigan+News+Service+-+Videos+Podcasts++Slideshows.

Morrison, K., 2015. Survey: Many Users Never Read Social Networking Terms of Service Agreements. *AdWeek*. [online]. Available at: http://adweek.it/1HMl9Wq.

Pagliery, J., 2016. Hackers Selling 117 Million LinkedIn Passwords. *CNN*. [online]. Available at: http://money.cnn.com/2016/05/19/technology/linkedin-hack/.

Peachey, K., 2015. Online Banking Fraud 'up by 48%'. *BBC News*. [online] 27 Mar. Available at: www.bbc.co.uk/news/business-32083781.

Robinson, D. and Ahmed, M., 2015. US Tech Companies Overhaul Operations after EU Data Ruling. *Financial Times*. [online]. Available at: www.ft.com/cms/s/0/5d75e65a-6bf8–11e5-aca9-d87542bf8673.htm.

Rogers, E.M., 2003. *Diffusion of Innovations*. 5th rev. ed. New York: Simon & Schuster International.

Ross, E., 2016. *Voices Heard Coming from Baby Monitors as Parents Are Warned of Hacks. The Independent*. [online]. Available at: www.independent.co.uk/life-style/gadgets-and-tech/news/baby-monitors-hacked-parents-warned-to-be-vigilant-after-voices-heard-coming-from-speakers-a6843346.html.

Rouhani-Arani, K., 2015. *The Internet of Things and Privacy in Europe and the USA. Taylor Wessing*. [online]. Available at: https://united-kingdom.taylorwessing.com/globaldatahub/article_wp29_iot.html.

Schwab, K., Marcus, A., Oyola, J., Hoffmann, W. and Luzi, M., 2011. *Personal Data: The Emergence of a New Asset Class*. Geneva: World Economic Forum.

Standage, T., 1999. *The Victorian Internet*. New ed. London: W&N.

Statista, 2016. *Mobile Phone Users Worldwide 2013–2019, Statistic. Statista*. [online]. Available at: www.statista.com/statistics/274774/forecast-of-mobile-phone-users-worldwide/.

Storm, D., 2014. Black Hat: Nest Thermostat Turned into a Smart Spy in 15 Seconds. *ComputerWorld*. [online]. Available at: www.computerworld.com/article/2476599/cybercrime-hacking/black-hat-nest-thermostat-turned-into-a-smart-spy-in-15-seconds.html.

Twentyman, J., 2016. *No Safe Harbour? Confusion Still Reigns Over EU-US Privacy Deal. Financial Times*. [online]. Available at: www.ft.com/cms/s/2/34d27d1c-ef4c-11e5–9f20-c3a047354386.html.

Versprille, A., 2015. Researchers Hack into Driverless Car System, Take Control of Vehicle. *National Defense Magazine*. [online]. Available at: www.nationaldefensemagazine.org/archive/2015/May/Pages/ResearchersHackIntoDriverlessCarSystemTakeControlofVehicle.aspx.

Walker, T., 2015. The Austrian Law Graduate Who became a Champion of Facebook Users. *The Independent*. [online]. Available at: www.independent.co.uk/

life-style/gadgets-and-tech/news/max-schrems-the-austrian-law-graduate-who-became-a-champion-of-facebook-users-a6683711.html.

WEF, 2016. Our Mission. *World Economic Forum.* [online]. Available at: www.weforum.org/about/world-economic-forum/.

Wolpin, S., 2014. The First Cellphone Went on Sale 30 Years Ago for $4,000. *Mashable.* [online]. Available at: http://mashable.com/2014/03/13/first-cellphone-on-sale/.

Zetter, K., 2016. Inside the Cunning, Unprecedented Hack of Ukraine's Power Grid. *WIRED.* [online]. Available at: www.wired.com/2016/03/inside-cunning-unprecedented-hack-ukraines-power-grid/.

7 The new business landscape

Introduction

The Internet of Things is a natural evolution of the innovation trajectories which the computing and telecommunications industries have been following for the previous 30 years. Computing devices have become smaller, more powerful and cheaper, and the networks for sharing data have become faster and more pervasive. The two industries and their technologies have converged to the extent that the 'information society' researchers such as Bell (1976), Stonier (1983) and Toffler (1970) predicted in the 1970s and 1980s has come to pass, although, perhaps, not quite in the ways they predicted. While governments have played a vital role in providing the environments and background infrastructure for the internet as we know it today, it is businesses which have created the products and services which have driven adoption on a mass scale. The previous chapters have considered the underpinning technologies of the IoT and the associated technical, business, legal and social challenges they pose. This concluding chapter brings together the intertwined threads discussed in previous chapters and considers their impact on the broader business landscape. The IoT will obviously have a significant effect on the technology sectors, but it also, as we have seen, cuts across other industries and has the potential to be transformative in the ways that businesses and the environments they operate in are structured. Some of these transformations are already under way, powered by the mass adoption of computing and communication technologies. While there is a danger of overemphasising the role of technology in social and economic transformation, the evidence of sustained and significant changes to business value chains resulting from new technologies is compelling. It is likely we are in the early stages of these changes and have yet to see their full impact.

Business winners

The IoT abounds with forecasts about the number of devices which will be connected, the profits which will be generated and the economic benefits to society. Consultants McKinsey & Co. predict a potential $11.1 trillion economic impact on the global economy by 2025 (Manyika et al., 2015), technology analyst IDC forecasts market revenues for IoT firms of $7 trillion by 2020 (IDC, 2014) and IoT analyst Machina Research sees almost 40 billion connected devices generating this value by 2024 (Machina Research, 2015). These are just a few of the predictions, and the ranges vary considerably. However, as we have seen, there is sufficient evidence to show that an underpinning IoT infrastructure is being built and devices are being connected to the extent that the IoT is becoming a reality. The chapter on business models discussed where the value is likely to be created in terms of profits by companies with the focus being on the data rather than necessarily the 'things' themselves. Just as oil formed the basis of a transport and energy revolution in the twentieth century, so data is seen as powering the next economic transformation which some are calling the Fourth Industrial Revolution (Schwab, 2016). While data may be the "new oil",[1] as Michael Palmer from the Association of National Advertisers rightly points out:

> Data is just like crude. It's valuable, but if unrefined it cannot really be used. It has to be changed into gas, plastic, chemicals, etc to create a valuable entity that drives profitable activity; so must data be broken down, analysed for it to have value.
>
> (Arthur, 2013)

If we accept the premise that data will underpin value creation in the emerging IoT world, then a key question is, which companies or types of companies will be those which will profit the most from this scenario? It is likely to be those further along the value chain where the data has already been captured and requires analysis which will benefit most. These include the large technology companies such as IBM with its Watson IoT platform which applies machine learning and natural language processing techniques to gain insights from unstructured data. This is a cloud-based application which offers customers the ability to pay as you go rather than the high upfront pricing structures often required for high-end business data processing services. IBM has positioned its Watson Platform as a key part of its strategy as it moves away from hardware services into software. By mid-2015, more than 77,000 active developers were using Watson and 100 companies were selling products built using the Watson developer platform (Chang and Chao, 2015). Google's DeepMind may also become a contender in the IoT data analytics space by applying its neural network technology to make sense of vast data sets.

Slightly further back on the IoT value chain are services such as Amazon Web Services (AWS) and Microsoft Azure which provide cloud-based platforms for data storage and processing. While not as sophisticated as IBM Watson or Google DeepMind in their ability to draw insights from unstructured data, they are becoming platforms for developers to build IoT software services. AWS will generate more than $10 billion for its parent company in 2016 and be responsible for more than half of total profits (Asay, 2016).

While the large data analytics companies are already generating significant revenues and profits from the IoT, it is not clear which companies further down the value chain and technology stack will be longer-term winners. It is quite possible that companies with a track record in the domestic space will be able to benefit if the smart home becomes a reality. However, as we saw in Chapter 4, the competencies needed to make IoT devices for households are not always the same as those needed to make less intelligent devices. Design and function are still important, but the IoT adds software and value-added services to the mix which some companies will struggle with. To combine these skillsets, it will be necessary for some companies to buy in these capabilities either through acquisitions such as Google's purchase of Nest or through partnerships.

Lessons learned from the evolution of the internet over the previous 20 years are certainly being applied by businesses in their IoT strategies. The realisation that stable technology standards are required for both innovators and users to have the confidence to invest in new products and services has long been recognised. This can be achieved through the market, via regulation or through the formation of consortia to establish common rules and protocols. In the smart home sector, the realisation that cooperation may be a good strategy was seen in 2016 with the announcement from Google that its Thread networking protocol would interoperate with software from the Open Connectivity Foundation (OCF). This follows Google's announcement earlier in 2016 that it would make Thread open source in a bid to encourage developers to adopt it as a standard. According to Grant Erickson, president of the Thread Group:

> In order for consumers to put their faith in the connected home, their experience must be simple, reliable, and effortless.
>
> (McCarthy, 2016)

Another lesson learned from the past 20 years of the internet is the importance of trust. Amazon and eBay have built hugely successful businesses by creating online marketplaces which buyers can trust via the system of user reviews of merchants and products. These companies have been able to build businesses which their customers have the confidence to share their credit card details with because Amazon and eBay are able to control their markets and remove traders and users who do not comply with their rules. Other parts of the internet have struggled more with this because there is no single company which can set and enforce the rules. Email provides a good example with levels of spam and fraudulent email scams threatening to destroy consumer trust in the service by the early 2000s. In 2005, a group of companies whose businesses relied on the successful take-up of email by consumers banded together to form the Online Trust Alliance (OTA). The founders included the Direct Marketing Association of the United States, Microsoft (owner of Hotmail and Outlook) and Symantec (an online security company). They realised that unless steps were taken to reduce spam levels and email fraud, users would move to other communication technologies. Since 2005, the OTA has worked with regulators and industry bodies to develop best practice guidelines to reduce spam levels as well as extend their operations into building consumer confidence in other areas of the internet. In 2015, the OTA formed the IoT Trustworthy Working Group (ITWG), which aims to do the same for the IoT and help manufacturers and service providers work to industry best practice with a focus on encouraging "security and privacy by design" (OTA, 2016). The nature of the information passing over the IoT means the risks of personal data misuse are much higher than email. Whether industry cooperation via formal and informal consortia will be sufficient to mitigate these risks or whether new legislation will be required remains to be seen.

Emerging technologies

At the same time as the IoT starts to gain traction, so do other potentially complementary technologies. These include artificial intelligence, machine learning and the blockchain.

The creation of artificial intelligence (AI) based on computing technologies has been dreamt of since the first days of the electronic computer. Early hopes that computers would be able to replicate the human characteristics of reasoning, learning and problem solving within a few years were not realised, but recent developments indicate they are getting closer. Since the 1990s, computers have consistently beaten humans in chess matches, and in March 2016, Google's AlphaGo computer beat the world champion of Go, a complex Chinese board game. The complexity of the game led many computing experts to believe it would take a decade for any company to build a computer capable of winning (Murray Brown, 2016). The AlphaGo computer was developed by Google DeepMind, which uses AI techniques to learn as it plays against competitors. However, computer scientists are quick to point out that what many call AI is more accurately defined as machine learning. AI in its purest forms refers to systems which are able to replicate human thought processes and exhibit signs of consciousness. We are a long way from this becoming a reality, but machine learning which uses algorithms to parse data, learn from it and make a prediction about something is already here (Copeland, 2016). These techniques are already being applied in IoT backend services through applications such as IBM Watson. Machine learning techniques are also used widely across the internet by companies such as Amazon for its suggestions of what to buy based on previous purchases and streaming music services which recommend tracks based on previous listening behaviour. The potential for AI/machine learning technologies to revolutionise what the IoT can offer business and broader society are immense. Making sense of historical data to better understand why systems behave the way they do is important and can help organisations with their strategic planning. However, the ability for systems to make sense of data in real time and predict problems before they occur presents exciting new possibilities. As tracking sensors are deployed across a range of industrial processes and within cities, this is starting to become a reality. As the director of digital learning at MIT, Professor Sanjay Sarma believes that:

> All technologies converge. It's inevitable. The benefits, in my view, are potentially incredible regarding the IoT. The BP disaster – imagine if AI were watching over those systems and could have detected the disaster earlier.
>
> (Meek, 2015)

Many believe that without more sophisticated machine learning techniques and, ultimately, AI being applied, the full potential of the IoT will not be realised (Jaffe, 2014). Some IoT technologies such as driverless cars and military systems will need the capability to apply AI in real time to the data they gather so they can respond to unexpected situations. This will require devices to be able to analyse data on the fly and without the support of cloud-based processing, which would take too long. The US defence research agency, DARPA, is experimenting with these approaches for its drones and other sensor-based devices which are used in the field to track hostile activity (Shah, 2016).

Early enthusiasts for the internet saw it as a network which would have a democratising effect on societies as information was wrestled away from the control of large corporations and governments and put in the hands, or computers, of individuals (Kelly, 1995; Locke, Searls and Weinberger, 1999). While the exchange of information has certainly become more fluid thanks to the internet, the dreams of a decentralised, information-based economy do not appear much closer. The old information gatekeepers of the mass media age have been replaced by new ones in the form of Google, Facebook, YouTube and Twitter. However, a new technology, the blockchain, is seen by many as having the potential to deliver on the promise of a decentralised, virtually friction-free, information society:

> A decentralised technology (the blockchain) will telegraph a decentralised world. . . . The blockchain's raison d'être is to enable us to imagine a new world that will be largely decentralized.
>
> (Mougayar, 2016, p.147)

So what is the blockchain and what relevance might it have to the IoT? At a technical level, the blockchain is complex and is based on mathematical principles. Essentially it is a technology which uses a distributed architecture and complex mathematical calculations to create a public ledger of transactions which cannot, in practical terms at least, be duplicated. It is the underpinning technology of Bitcoin, the digital asset and payment system created by Satoshi Nakamoto[2] in 2009. In the case of Bitcoin, the blockchain technology powering it provides a database of every transaction which takes place using the currency. While it may seem an esoteric technology with little application for the real world, many see the blockchain as a revolutionary technology as or more significant than the underpinning technologies of the internet such as TCP/IP, SMTP and FTP. Using blockchain technology to authenticate online transactions, it is claimed, will radically reduce transaction costs by removing expensive gatekeepers such as financial institutions and public bodies such as land registries. There is certainly much interest in the blockchain as an enabling technology with, perhaps ironically, some of the biggest investors in blockchain initiatives coming from the banking industry. Global technology consulting firm PwC has developed a consulting practice offering blockchain development services to its clients and sees the technology offering a radical solution to all types of business:

> Imagine being able to transfer value or prevent contractual disputes over the Internet – without going through a third party. Confidently. Securely. Almost instantly. This is the promise of blockchain based technology. The implications are so profound that its implementation could revolutionize business practices as we know them.
>
> (PricewaterhouseCoopers, 2016)

While PwC may have an agenda to promote the blockchain as a new way of generating client business and revenue for itself, the technology does offer real potential for the IoT. Microsoft offers what it calls Blockchain as a service (BaaS) on its Azure platform which is widely used by IoT developers. It sees the secure authentication capabilities of the blockchain as ideal for IoT applications which need to make secure transactions, particularly where these are financial transactions. IBM similarly offers a cloud-based blockchain solution for IoT developers via its Bluemix IoT platform. While the current state of blockchain usage in IoT applications is still at the development/conceptual stage, real uses for this technology have been envisaged. These include using the blockchain to give vending machines and washing machines the autonomy to automatically order new supplies when running low and solicit bids from the cheapest suppliers. Papleux (2016) sees the blockchain as providing the much needed level of security essential for machine-to-machine financial transactions that will support take-up of the IoT across a number of industries. Technology consultants Accenture have developed a proof of concept IoT electric plug which can autonomously shop around for the cheapest electricity supply deals and pay for the energy using Bitcoin (Cellan-Jones, 2016).

IoT and employment

While vending machines which automatically replenish themselves and factory production lines which can order their own supplies may be an attractive cost-saving measure for firms, they also have the potential to threaten the jobs of people who have traditionally done these things. New technologies have been seen as a threat to workers since the eighteenth century, when water- and steam-powered factories revolutionised the production of many types of goods. In the latter half of the twentieth century, computing technologies made much clerical work obsolete and, it is argued, we are entering a new phase of technological development where many skilled jobs will also be at risk.

Brynjolfsson and McAfee (2012) contend that the rapid development of new computing technologies such as artificial intelligence and machine learning are transforming industries and creating new business models. While the effect of this for consumers is often the development of cheaper goods and services, the impact on jobs is not so positive:

> Computers are only going to get more powerful and capable in the future, and have an ever-bigger impact on jobs, skills and the economy. The root of our problems is not that we're in a Great Recession or a Great Stagnation, but rather that we're in the early throes of a Great Restructuring. Our technologies are racing ahead but many of our skills and organizations are lagging behind.
>
> (Brynjolfsson and McAfee, 2012, p.9)

The authors believe that while productivity in the United States has generally been on an upward trajectory since the 1970s, median household incomes have not risen accordingly. A large part of this, they claim, is due to the application of computing and communication technologies within the workplace, which has made organisations more productive and, therefore profitable, but not passed this increase on to workers. The replacement of skilled workers by computing technologies can be seen in the legal profession and the process of 'discovery' in corporate law. This traditionally involves lawyers reading through many thousands of pages of corporate documents to look for evidence which can be used in disputes. The application of AI software to sort through digital copies of documents is a reality and a job which, according to Sobowale (2016), would have taken three people six months to complete can now be done in several days. Founder of the World Economic Forum (WEF), Klaus Schwab (2016), believes the IoT will result in job losses for many, particularly at the unskilled end, but that there will also be many benefits to society in terms of better use of natural resources and safety in the workplace.

Whatever the impact the IoT has on employment, it is at too early a stage of development to know for sure. The application of computers in the workplace did make some roles redundant, but it also created new jobs which had not previously existed such as database managers, system support and application developers. The hope will be that more new jobs are created by the IoT than are made obsolete.

Notes

1 The phrase "data is the new oil" is attributed to Clive Humby from a talk he gave at the Association of National Advertisers senior marketers' summit, Kellogg School, in 2006 (Palmer, 2006). Along with Edwina Dunn, Clive Humby helped Tesco create the Tesco Clubcard in the mid-1990s, which transformed how retailers gathered data on their customers for loyalty schemes.

2 Satoshi Nakamoto is a pseudonym used by the creator of Bitcoin. Although some people claim to know who the inventor is, as of August 2016 his/her/their real name(s) is/are not publicly known.

References

Arthur, C., 2013. Tech Giants May Be Huge, but Nothing Matches Big Data. *The Guardian.* [online] 23 Aug. Available at: www.theguardian.com/technology/2013/aug/23/tech-giants-data.

Asay, M., 2016. Amazon CFO Said These 3 Factors Are the Reason for AWS Revenue Explosion. *TechRepublic*. [online]. Available at: www.techrepublic.com/article/amazon-cfo-said-these-3-factors-are-the-reason-for-aws-revenue-explosion/.

Bell, D., 1976. *The Coming of Post-Industrial Society*. New ed. New York: Basic Books.

Brynjolfsson, E. and McAfee, A., 2012. *Race against the Machine: How the Digital Revolution Is Accelerating Innovation, Driving Productivity, and Irreversibly Transforming Employment and the Economy*. Lexington, MA: Digital Frontier Press.

Cellan-Jones, R., 2016. Bitcoin Could Help Cut Power Bills. *BBC News*. [online] 19 Feb. Available at: www.bbc.co.uk/news/technology-35604674.

Chang, E. and Chao, J., 2015. Watson Set to Become 'Huge Engine' for Sales, IBM Executive Says. *Bloomberg*. [online]. Available at: www.bloomberg.com/news/articles/2015–09–24/watson-set-to-become-huge-engine-for-sales-ibm-executive-says.

Copeland, M., 2016. The Difference between AI, Machine Learning, and Deep Learning. *The Official NVIDIA Blog*. [online]. Available at: https://blogs.nvidia.com/blog/2016/07/29/whats-difference-artificial-intelligence-machine-learning-deep-learning-ai/.

IDC, 2014. *IDC Market in a Minute: Internet of Things*. [online]. Available at: www.idc.com/downloads/idc_market_in_a_minute_iot_infographic.pdf.

Jaffe, M., 2014. IoT Won't Work Without Artificial Intelligence. *WIRED*. [online]. Available at: www.wired.com/insights/2014/11/iot-wont-work-without-artificial-intelligence/.

Kelly, K., 1995. *Out of Control: The New Biology of Machines, Social Systems, and the Economic World*. Reading, MA: Basic Books.

Locke, C., Searls, D. and Weinberger, D., 1999. *The Cluetrain Manifesto*. London: FT.

Machina Research, 2015. Successful Monetization of the Internet of Things Will Bring a $1.3 Trillion Reward. *Machina Research*. [online]. Available at: https://machinaresearch.com/report/successful-monetization-of-the-internet-of-things-will-bring-a-13-trillion-reward/.

Manyika, J., Chui, M., Bisson, P., Woetzel, J., Dobbs, R., Bughin, J. and Aharon, D., 2015. *The Internet of Things: Mapping the Value beyond the Hype*. San Francisco, CA: McKinsey & Company.

McCarthy, K., 2016. Google-Backed Thread, OCF Form Alliance for Internet of Things Sanity. *The Register*. [online]. Available at: www.theregister.co.uk/2016/08/01/thread_and_ocf_form_alliance_for_iot_sanity/.

Meek, A., 2015. Connecting Artificial Intelligence with the Internet of Things. *The Guardian*. [online] 24 Jul. Available at: www.theguardian.com/technology/2015/jul/24/artificial-intelligence-internet-of-things.

Mougayar, W., 2016. *The Business Blockchain: Promise, Practice, and Application of the Next Internet Technology*. Hoboken, NJ: Wiley.

Murray Brown, J., 2016. Google DeepMind Computer Beats Go Grandmaster Again. *Financial Times*. [online]. Available at: www.ft.com/cms/s/0/38b6f0c4-e6a1–11e5-bc31–138df2ae9ee6.html.

OTA, 2016. *Internet of Things*. *Online Trust Alliance*. [online]. Available at: https://otalliance.org/initiatives/internet-things.

Palmer, M., 2006. Data Is the New Oil. *ANA Marketing Maestros*. [online]. Available at: http://ana.blogs.com/maestros/2006/11/data_is_the_new.html.

Papleux, F., 2016. Blockchain Technology to Solve Internet of Things Problems – Accenture. *Accenture Blog*. [online]. Available at: www.accenture.com/us-en/blogs/blogs-using-blockchain-solve-internet-things-problems.

PricewaterhouseCoopers, 2016. PwC's Blockchain Services. *PwC.* [online]. Available at: www.pwc.com/us/en/financial-services/fintech/blockchain.html.
Schwab, K., 2016. *The Fourth Industrial Revolution.* Geneva: World Economic Forum.
Shah, A., 2016. DARPA Sees IoT and AI as Weapons to Dominate Wars. *PCWorld.* [online]. Available at: www.pcworld.com/article/3114116/darpa-sees-iot-and-ai-as-weapons-to-dominate-wars.html.
Sobowale, J., 2016. How Artificial Intelligence Is Transforming the Legal Profession. *ABA Journal.* [online]. Available at: www.abajournal.com/magazine/article/how_artificial_intelligence_is_transforming_the_legal_profession/.
Stonier, T., 1983. *The Wealth of Information: Profile of the Post-industrial Society.* London: Mandarin.
Toffler, A., 1970. *Future shock.* New York: Random House.

Index

Printed in the United States
by Baker & Taylor Publisher Services